THE PHILOSOPHY
OF SARTRE

Philosophy

———

Editor

PROFESSOR H. J. PATON
MA, FBA, D.LITT, LL.D
Emeritus Professor of Moral Philosophy
in the University of Oxford

THE PHILOSOPHY
OF SARTRE

Mary Warnock

HUTCHINSON UNIVERSITY LIBRARY
LONDON

HUTCHINSON & CO (*Publishers*) LTD
178–202 Great Portland Street, London W1

London Melbourne Sydney
Auckland Bombay Toronto
Johannesburg New York

First published 1965
Second impression 1966

Undergraduate Lending Library
© Mary Warnock 1965

This book has been set in Times, printed in Great Britain
on Smooth Wove paper by Anchor Press, and
bound by Wm. Brendon, both of Tiptree, Essex

Contents

Acknowledgment

The extracts from *L'Etre et le Néant*
and *La Nausée* are translated by kind
permission of M. Jean-Paul Sartre.

Preface

In this book I have not attempted to discuss anything but Sartre's philosophy. Both in the field of philosophy and in that of literature Sartre has written what would represent a whole life's work for a normal man, and though his work is closely integrated, it seems to me that the first task of a commentator on it is to select. It is easy for the reader to get lost in the formidable number of words that he has written. Moreover, to understand Sartre's contributions to literature it is absolutely necessary to have some grasp of his philosophical commitments. So this study may be taken as an introduction to the whole of Sartre's work.

Even within the area of philosophy a great deal of selection has seemed to me necessary; and it may be thought that I have spent too much time on mere exposition, at the expense of criticism and analysis. To this charge I would answer that Sartre's philosophical writings present a peculiar problem to the reader. He is extraordinarily obscure and repetitive, so that it is more than usually necessary for someone who is going to try to treat him seriously as a philosopher to have some guidance—even though he may well dissent from his guide, and may decide to go by other landmarks and signposts in the end. Furthermore, a detailed, sentence-by-sentence analysis of any one of Sartre's philosophical writings would come to no good. For his method of composition is cumulative. He often attempts three or four ways of conveying a certain impression, which do not necessarily say exactly the same as, and may even contradict, each other. Almost everything he says about, for instance, perception could be discussed and probably quarrelled with. But if one did that one would mistake his purpose; for, regrettably perhaps, he does not want to be precise, nor to get things exactly right. He is interested in presenting a picture of what things are like, in bludgeoning his readers into accepting a certain view of the world, and he does not care very much what weapons he uses to do this. Above everything else his philosophical method is descriptive. He aims to present an absolutely complete description of the world in its most general aspects; so that he is a metaphysician, but essentially a literary metaphysician.

He is also an existentialist, or at least for a time he was one. This means that his descriptions are for the most part designed to convey a certain definite thesis about human freedom, and a thesis which is supposed to have a practical bearing on how to live. Human beings, alone of all the objects in the universe, have to make free choices, and the range of their freedom is immense. They are free not only to do as they choose but to feel as they choose—in short, to *be* whatever they choose. With this extreme belief in freedom goes an equally extreme pessimism about the human predicament. It is probably true that all serious moral philosophers have been recognizably optimistic or recognizably pessimistic. I would argue that Sartre is to be taken seriously as a moral philosopher, even though what he actually says about moral theory is a minute part of his philosophy as a whole. He attempts to deduce it, as all metaphysical moral theorists do, from a general view of the place of man in nature, and it is this view which, in his case, is deeply pessimistic. He believes that a philosopher should be able to answer the question 'What ought we to do?'; but the answer that he gives seems to be that there is nothing that we can do, or at least nothing that we can do as individuals, that will not be futile.

But it would be misleading to present this as the end of the story. For Sartre has gone on developing; and in his latest book there are signs that he may ultimately have some more hopeful answer to the question of what people should do, and how they should live. For in the end he has given up existentialism; and in the last chapter of this book I have tried to show how his new doctrines arise out of his old ones. In a way it must be admitted that such an attempt is ill-timed, since the latest book, *The Critique of Dialectical Reason*, is only half completed. But it is safe to say that, for the time being at least, Sartre has become more interested in sociology than in philosophy, and that such solutions as he offers will be in terms of how people should live in groups. He thinks now of men, not as a part of the whole natural order, but as essentially conditioned by their membership of human groups and classes. I am aware that I have dealt very briefly in this book with the *Critique*. The sociological doctrines which it contains are still being hammered out, and their relevance to other subjects, such as literary criticism and history, is still emerging. I hope, all the same, that the present book may serve not only as a guide to what Sartre has already written but as a partial introduction to what he has still to write.

I must finally repeat the warning that I am concerned chiefly with philosophy, which has perhaps always been something of a side-line for Sartre himself.

One may therefore raise the question whether it is worth the trouble to try to sort out Sartre's philosophical views. It may be argued that he is not primarily a philosopher, or not that alone, and that there are many more original thinkers with the discussion of whom one would be better employed. It is true that Sartre is not an original thinker, and it is for this reason that it is impossible to discuss his philosophy at all without doing something to present its origins and the history which lies behind it. But this is not a bad way of doing philosophy in any case. There is very seldom a philosopher of such genius that he succeeds in asking new philosophical questions. Most philosophers attempt only to give true answers to old questions, and in order to understand them it is essential to understand something of how the questions were first asked and answered. Sartre takes over not only the questions but a great deal of the terminology for answering them, and even the answers themselves, from his predecessors; and a far longer book than this would be needed to expound the sources, mainly in German idealism, from which his ideas have been drawn. But what makes it worth trying to follow his thought, during its long and tortuous journey from Hegel through Husserl to Marx, is the highly individual and personal flavour which his writing has. Perhaps this is only to say that in the end Sartre is a literary not a philosophical giant. But such distinctions are not very important. By the time we come to the end of *Being and Nothingness* Sartre has got us to see the world through his eyes. It is impossible not to feel that the struggle was worth while, even if one has learned only what it is like to be so splendidly and romantically desperate. It is inevitably disappointing that after this vision he seems to present us with a not very attractive way out—to become Marxists. And our disappointment is undoubtedly greater because of the almost impossible difficulty of reading the latest book, in which all the worst features of French and German philosophical writing seem to have come together to produce a book which must tax the perseverence of the most enthusiastic, and in which, of his earlier philosophical style, only the seemingly deliberate obscurity is left. I believe that it is positively *wrong* to write in such a way.

However, it is still true that we want to find out what Sartre says, and what he is going to say next. Accordingly, throughout this book my aim has been to clarify, though I am aware that I have often failed. For the remaining obscurities, as well as for misinterpretation, I apologize to my readers, and more especially to Sartre himself.

I am very grateful to Mrs. John North for her translations.

1

Cartesianism

(1) 'Cogito ergo sum'

Sartre, like all French philosophers, treats Descartes as the father of the subject, and 'Cogito ergo sum', Descartes' supposedly indubitable foundation for his whole system, as somehow containing the germ of all truth within itself. He is not wrong to think of Cartesianism as fruitful in a quite peculiar way; but this very fruitfulness means that we, as students of Sartre, need not worry very much about what Descartes himself meant, or even what he said. His words have been interpreted in many different ways, and it will be enough for us to see what Sartre made of them. For from the seminal ideas which he found in Descartes, Sartre may be said to have developed the two main thoughts which dominate his whole philosophical development, at least up to his latest book. Up to the time of the revolutionary *Critique of Dialectical Reason* his philosophy rests on the twin pillars of human freedom and human powers of self-analysis. These are the main themes of *Being and Nothingness*, and even his political ideas may be seen in some sense to derive from these.

'Cogito ergo sum' is a statement of immediate self-awareness. Sartre elaborates this self-awareness in two different ways. In the first place, part of what is denoted by 'cogitatio' is the will. Descartes supposes us to have an immediate apprehension of our own will; that is, of our power to choose and to decide. An immediate awareness of our own freedom is thus taken to be a part of the indubitable foundation for all thought and all action. Secondly, 'cogitatio' means thinking about things. We are immediately

13

aware of ideas in our minds, and these ideas are somehow related to the outside world. So, by inspecting our own consciousness, we can learn what can and cannot be known, and in what manner whatever we know is known. And since all we know is, according to Descartes, our ideas, and since these are in our consciousness, we know, at the same time as we know our ideas, something about that consciousness in which they are. We know our own minds better than anything else. This second interpretation of the 'cogito' led Sartre to phenomenology, and the reflective concentration on what consciousness is actually like.

(2) Awareness of freedom

In 1946 Sartre published an introduction to a selection of the writings of Descartes, which is an interesting example in itself of his characteristic method of criticism—personal, loaded, and full of insights. In this introduction the first interpretation of the 'cogito', as awareness of freedom, is expounded. Descartes, he says, was immediately aware of freedom in the act of judging. This immediate awareness is shared by any student of mathematics, who learns to take off by himself, leaving the guidance of his teacher, and who realizes that if he gives his whole mind to the matter and is not distracted he can work the problems out for himself. What he has to give to the task is 'esprit' or 'mens'; everything, that is, which is not his body.

Descartes realizes better than anyone, Sartre says, the autonomy of thought. But this feature is quite different from the productiveness, or creativity, of thought, though these are its characteristics as well. In the *Discourse* Descartes did not concentrate on creativity. He was interested above all in mathematical learning, where there are fixed rules of procedure and, though the mind is free to go on alone, it must go on according to given rules. Descartes thought, according to Sartre, that the mind could not exercise creative freedom when occupied either with mathematical or scientific subjects, for a man cannot *invent* for himself the rules of mathematics or the rules of thought in general. He can be creatively free only in imaginative thinking. What kind of freedom is left for thought, then, in mathematics and science? Men may still be said to be free, Descartes says, to reject the false, to say 'no' to what is not the truth. This *is* freedom, and it secures that autonomy of thought which he intuited at the beginning.

But Sartre is not satisfied with this solution. Is this power to reject the false enough to give us the powerful and immediate awareness of freedom which we were supposed to have in the 'cogito'? Sartre thinks that it is not, and that Descartes was guilty of confusion at this point. He has, Sartre maintains, two senses of 'freedom', and he switches from one to the other as it suits him. The first sense is that in which a man is aware that he is *actively* free—free, that is, to act, to judge, to comprehend, and to create; the second sense is that in which man is free only to avoid error, and this is the sense upon which Descartes falls back, when he is concerned merely to preserve the autonomy of thought in the face of the rigorousness of pre-existing rules. He tends to amalgamate the two senses when he talks of man's responsibility when faced with the truth. He sometimes speaks as though, unless I make a judgment, a free act, there is no truth. But this is not really compatible with the example of a child learning to apply the rules of arithmetic, which hold whether the child can apply them or not.

Whether or not there is in Descartes this double use of the word 'free' as applied to thought is a question which need not concern us. But Sartre certainly believes that he can find two senses, and that both are important. Indeed, both senses turn out to be essential to his own view of human freedom. In the active or creative sense we *know* that we are free, and the fact that we can think what we choose is proof of it; it is further proved each time we perform any action whatever. In the other, non-creative, sense we are free to deny, if not to assert; to reject, if not to accept. And here we have come upon what, in Sartre's own theory, is the most important characteristic of human consciousness, indeed that which uniquely marks it off from beings of all other kinds—namely, its power to deny, to conceive the opposite of what is presented to it, and to think of the present situation in terms of what is not the case. In neither of these two senses does Sartre think that human freedom can possibly be denied.

To return to the exposition of Descartes: Sartre says that Descartes is at every moment asserting his own freedom of thought in his denial of the scholastic doctrine of essences upon which he had been brought up, and which amounted to imprisonment. He is freely giving his own assent, and that of his readers, to the laws of nature, and rejecting the false constructions which he had been taught. In the fourth *Meditation* he argues that his will, by which he assents to the laws of nature, is the very same as God's will, by which they were first created. What distinguishes God from man is not greater freedom but greater power. Freedom in this negative sense is limitless for men and is expressed in their rejection of false versions of natural laws and their acceptance of the true. (Rather quaintly, Sartre therefore finds in Descartes' scientific doctrines the foundation of democracy. 'No one realizes better than Descartes the connexion between the scientific and the democratic spirit.' The system of universal suffrage can be founded on, and justified by, only the universal freedom to accept or reject, to say 'yes' or 'no'.)

But freedom in the creative sense is not limitless, in Descartes' view. For even in his own case, where he is freely inventing the laws of scientific discovery, the rigours of the pre-established order intervene. Thus, Sartre argues, even the freedom of invention which Descartes does ascribe to men is not satisfactory. For Descartes brings together his two kinds of freedom—the limitless freedom to deny the false and the limited freedom to invent rules—and in the amalgamation he speaks as though even the rules which we freely invent are somehow *suggested* to us in virtue of their being right. Thus we are totally free to accept or to reject the false: but the true and the right are, in some sense, *given* to us. And, Sartre says, 'If man does not invent his own Good, if he does not construct his own science, he is only nominally free.'

Descartes ascribes total creative freedom—freedom to invent the good and the true—to God, along with His limitless power. And so Sartre says that Descartes has ascribed to God what should properly have been ascribed to man. However, Descartes should not be reproached for this; for his great contribution to the truth was to see that, whether one speaks of God or of man, freedom is the 'sole foundation of being', and that we must be aware of freedom in being aware that we exist. In Sartre's own view the very freedom to accept or reject the false is itself creative. Our power to envisage what is not the case leads to our power to change what is. The one could not exist without the other. This is a characteristically Sartrean extension of the Cartesian views propounded in the introduction to the *Selection*. We shall have much more to say in a later chapter about Sartre's doctrine of human freedom. But it is time, for the moment, to examine the other aspect of his broad interpretation of Descartes.

(3) Self-consciousness

Besides the concept of human freedom as something of which we are necessarily directly aware, Sartre claims to derive from Descartes a certain view of human consciousness in general. Indeed, it is to this view of consciousness that he himself is most inclined to award the honorific title of Cartesianism. Roughly, the view is that human consciousness must always be directed upon some object of which it will be aware; but that, further, in being aware of this object, it will also be aware of itself perceiving, or being aware. Sometimes the object of awareness will be something in the world, sometimes it will be the self. But in either case it will always be accompanied by an awareness of being aware. This second-order awareness is referred to by Sartre as 'the pre-reflective cogito'.

From the proposition that consciousness always is, or can be, conscious of itself, various things follow. One, the importance of which as a recurring theme in Sartre's philosophical psychology will emerge later, is a strong opposition to Freudianism. For if consciousness is defined as that which is aware of itself, the notion of the unconscious can have no possible place in psychology.

The second consequence, however, is our immediate concern. Given the existence of 'the pre-reflective cogito', it must always be possible to describe what consciousness is like, and, if there are different modes of consciousness, to describe these different modes. For since consciousness operates always at two levels at once it must, with sufficient care and patience, be possible to construct a kind of running commentary on what consciousness is doing at any particular moment. The description of different modes of our consciousness of the world plays an enormously important part in Sartre's philosophy. Indeed, the possibility of this kind of description is the foundation of *Being and Nothingness*, his first major philosophical work, and his best. But before *Being and Nothingness* the method was pursued in some detail, first in his studies of the imagination, and then in his *Sketch for a Theory of the Emotions*. It is to the examination of these works that the bulk of the present chapter will be devoted.

But first the question may be raised whether this descriptive psychology, upon which the philosophy of Sartre is founded, has in fact anything to do with the Cartesian tradition. To this the short answer is that it has not. Sartre's 'Cartesianism' is in fact not derived from Descartes at all, but from the German phenomenologists Brentano and Husserl—to whom, in fact, he acknowledges himself to be greatly indebted. Descartes, it is true, claimed to base his whole philosophy on his famous 'cogito' argument; but the uses to which he put it were very different. Having decided to trust neither his senses nor what he had learned from other people, he found that he could not doubt his own existence, whatever else he doubted; for he proved his own existence as a thinking being every time he doubted, or performed any other act of thought or cognition whatever. The basis of his system of philosophy, therefore, was the proposition that he existed as a thinking being. But from here he went on to argue that, *as* a thinking being, he had ideas of things. And the question which he had most urgently to solve was the question of what clue, if any, these ideas gave him to the external world. Did they truly represent things in the external world as they were? Or were they all of them deceptive? Ideas were, for him, existent things which could be inspected, and which must be tested carefully in order to find out whether they were true representations of the world, or false and misleading. By far the greatest contribution to the subsequent history of philosophy which Descartes made was the raising of this particular question in this particular form. Indeed, it would not be a great exaggeration to say that his problem, that of the relation of our ideas to the external world, dominated philosophical thought until the end of the nineteenth century. The phenomenologists were among the first to try to escape from the Cartesian prison.

Descartes' own solution to his problem was not nearly so important as his posing of it. Unadventurously, he answered that on the whole we can trust our ideas to be true representations of things, provided we take care to concentrate only upon clear and distinct ideas. Moreover, one of the ideas which we can quite certainly trust for its clarity and distinctness is the idea we have of a benevolent and non-deceptive God, who would not allow us to be perpetually deceived by our other ideas, and who on the whole guides us, even in our free inventions, towards the true rather than the false.

Besides these central arguments, however, in which Descartes concentrated on the separation between ideas and the objects of which they are representations in the mind, he argued, somewhat as an after-thought, that since all my knowledge comes to me through my mind, I must necessarily know my mind better than anything else—better, in particular, than my body or any other corporeal thing. Mental substance is luminous to itself as corporeal substance is not. Now this minor and highly dubious argument could perhaps be said to suggest the view of consciousness which we are considering here, for it might suggest that, at the same time as being aware of an object, I must also be aware of my mind perceiving that object. For instance, in *Meditation II* Descartes says: 'If the notion of perception of wax has seemed to me clearer and more distinct, not only after the sight and touch, but also after many other causes have rendered it quite manifest to me, with how much more evidence and distinctness must it be said that I now know myself, since all the reasons which contribute to the knowledge of wax or any other body whatever are yet better proofs of the nature of my mind. And there are so many other things in the mind itself which may contribute to the elucidation of its nature, that those which depend on body such as these just mentioned hardly merit being taken into account.' This was certainly the point upon which Husserl and the other phenomenologists fastened in their reading of Descartes. To understand Sartre's so-called Cartesianism it is necessary to try, very briefly, to state the main theses of phenomenology to which it is in fact so very closely related.

(4) Phenomenology

In 1874 Franz Brentano published a book called *Psychology from an Empirical Point of View*. This work can be said to be the beginning of descriptive psychology, although the spirit of Brentano's enquiry was in many ways reminiscent of Hume. His central doctrine was that *intentional existence* is the unique and defining characteristic of the mental; in other words, that all mental or psychological activities whatever are necessarily directed upon some object. But what peculiarly marks off mental from physical activities is that while, if physical activities have objects at all, these must exist; in the case of mental activities their objects need not exist. Thus I may equally well think about a golden mountain, which is the object of my thought and which does not exist, as about my gold watch, which does. This distinction led, in the writings of Meinong and elsewhere, to great differences of opinion about the kind of existence which must be ascribed to the golden mountain if it is to be an object, even an object of thought. But we need not pursue these discussions here. Brentano's aim was to provide a characterization of mental activities, or consciousness, which would make it intelligible to speak of describing consciousness itself, including its intentionality or direction upon an object, without necessarily being committed to describing, or even assigning existence to, the object itself. And he further believed that it was to the description of consciousness alone that philosophers ought to direct their attention.

Husserl wrote of Brentano's descriptive psychology thus: 'His conversion of the scholastic concept of intentionality into a descriptive root-concept of psychology constitutes a great discovery, apart from which phenomenology could not have come into being at all' (*Ideas: General introduction to pure Phenomenology*, p. 23). What then exactly is phenomenology, which thus depends on the intentionality of mental acts? The best short source for an answer to this question is to be found in the article under that heading, written by Husserl himself, in the fourteenth edition of the *Encyclopaedia Britannica*.

Essentially, phenomenology consists in the analysis of what is available to introspection in its generality, without making use of any extraneous knowledge of causes, or of natural laws which apply to the outside world, which the practiser of phenomenology may have. The phenomenologist, according to Husserl, sets aside his normal standpoint, or performs an *epoche*. He puts into brackets, that is, everything which, as an ordinary plain man, he may happen to know or to assume about what causes his experience. This is what Husserl means by saying that 'Phenomenology is *a priori* in the best sense of the word'. In describing his experience the phenomenologist does not get in any way involved in what he describes. He stands apart from it, and 'performs a phenomenological reduction to the facts themselves'. That is to say, he concentrates, as far as he can, upon the pure experience as he has it, without presuppositions or concepts derived from elsewhere than the experience itself. This is the essence of the method.

But before Husserl can embark on the actual descriptions of internal experience he has one problem which he has to clear up, that of the Self. He distinguished 'psychical' from 'transcendental' selfhood. The former is an empirical concept. The self in this sense is what is studied by ordinary introspection (if, for instance, one ordinarily reflects upon one's character or failings, one is concerned with the psychical self), by psychiatry, and even by history. The psychical self is in the world. Transcendental selfhood, on the other hand, is presupposed even in our most detailed description of ourselves in the psychical sense. It is what Wittgenstein later was to refer to as the 'non-psychological self', a limit, not a part of the world (*Tractatus Logico-Philosophicus*, 5.632).

There is, in this distinction, the difference we have already hinted at in Sartre between the 'pre-reflective cogito' (the transcendental self of Husserl) and the power of reflection, or reflexive awareness, in which the self can be thought of as an object to itself in introspection. The distinction is the same, and both Husserl and Sartre, who follow him, think of it as Cartesian. Husserl, however, goes on, as Sartre does not, to identify this transcendental self in some way with absolute being. Unlike Brentano, who thought that the philosopher's whole task was to be patiently descriptive, Husserl claimed that by performing the preliminary act of abstraction, and concentrating each upon his own consciousness, philosophers could reach a universal, absolute, and general truth. He believed that by means of the method of phenomenology an absolute and unified science could be achieved. Into this grandiose and largely unintelligible field of speculation we fortunately need not follow him, for Sartre certainly does not.

But however wide or narrow its claims, two features

stand out as essential to the phenomenological method. First, there is the often repeated injunction to perform a *reduction*—that is, to examine experience as it is internally presented to one. And secondly, following from this, the main task of philosophy will emerge as the discovery of the nature of the world *from a certain point of view*, as it is presented, that is to say, to *my* consciousness of myself, which goes along with, and contains, every experience of the world that I have. It is these features which constitute by far the most important heritage which existentialism in general, and Sartre's philosophy in particular, took over.

(5) Sartrean psychology

(a) *Imagination*
Let us now see how Sartre made use of this inheritance in his own descriptive psychology. His first interest was in the imagination. In 1936 he published a short introductory study of the subject under the title *L'imagination*, and this was followed in 1940 by a more elaborate and original work, *L'imaginaire*. The first has been translated under the title *The Imagination*, the second under the title *The Psychology of the Imagination*. In the introductory book Sartre's problem is to determine what images are, and what their relationship is to the things of which they are the images. His main aim in the discussion is to avoid the mistake, into which philosophers and psychologists nearly always fall, of treating images as a kind of *thing*. This mistake has, he thinks, bedevilled the whole of the philosophical treatment of the subject. However, it is far from clear that in the end Sartre manages to escape it himself, as we shall see.

He begins by giving an historical account of the problem of the image, criticizing the solutions of previous philosophers and ending with the solution proposed by Husserl. This is the characteristic pattern of all the early psychological treatises. He first divides the theories of the image current in the seventeenth and eighteenth centuries into three kinds. Unfortunately this historical chapter is in

Sartre's worst manner—unclear, and without exact references to the works of the philosophers whose views he is criticizing, though his criticisms are supposed to be directed against the specific views of specific people. All the theories discussed are characterized in so hopelessly abstract a manner that it is almost impossible to identify the theories and ascribe them to their proper authors. However, broadly speaking, the three theories which he distinguishes are these. First, there is the Cartesian belief that images are in some sense physical, perhaps parts of the brain, and that therefore to pass from talking about images to talking about thoughts is to take a great leap. They are categorially different things. Secondly, there is the belief, which Sartre ascribes to Hume, that images are all that there is. Our whole experience consists of impressions, and, while only some of these are called images, those so called are not different in kind from the rest of our experiences. (It might be thought that Berkeley would be a better example of a holder of this belief than Hume, but that does not matter.) Thirdly, there is the view of Spinoza and Leibniz that images are just very confused thoughts. Common to all these three views is the assumption that images are a kind of things.

Then, after analysing various later views—that of Taine, the associationists, and others—Sartre expounds the phenomenological view of Husserl, with which he claims to be in almost total agreement. Above all, Sartre admires Husserl's insistence that the first task is to discover what psychic phenomena in general are before going on to investigate them individually and in detail. He says: 'Psychology will make great strides when it ceases to burden itself with ambiguous and contradictory experiments and starts bringing to light the essential structures constituting the subject of its investigations.' The notion of intentionality, introduced by the phenomenologists, gives, he says, a new conception of images. 'An image, too, is an image *of something*. We are dealing therefore with a certain consciousness of a certain object. In a word, the image ceases to be a psychic *content*. It is not *in* the consciousness.' It is rather a part of consciousness or a mode of consciousness.

All this is contained in embryo in Husserl's theory, but, according to Sartre, the theory as it stands is incomplete. He says: 'We see now that an image and a perception are two different intentional *Erlebnisse*, distinguished above all by their intentions. But what is the nature of imaginative intending, and how does it differ from perceptual intending? A description of essences is evidently needed. Lacking any further account by Husserl, the task must fall on us.' And finally, on the last page of the book, he says: 'There are not, and never could be, images *in* consciousness. Rather an image is *a certain type of consciousness*. An image is an act, not something. An image is a consciousness *of* something. Our critical investigation cannot go further. A phenomenological description of the structure known as "an image" would have to be the next step.'

It is this kind of description which he sets about giving in *L'imaginaire*, published in 1940. This is a long and illuminating book, worth reading both for itself and as an introduction to *Being and Nothingness*. There is a great deal in it which is of interest to literary critics as well as to philosophers, and it is impossible to do it justice in a short summary. The work is divided into two parts; that which is certain, and that which is probable. The first part, the certain, is what is (supposedly) derived from phenomenological reflection. At this stage at least, Sartre seems to accept entirely the scientific claims which Husserl made for the method. The second part, the probable, is supposed to consist of deductions both from this reflection and from ordinary experimental data. But it must be said that this division into parts does not really work out very well; and in any case Sartre seems to state the probable with exactly the same degree of conviction, and the same amount of evidence, as he states the certain.

The book starts at the place where *L'imagination* left the subject. The difference between the perception of a chair and the imagination of a chair consists in the mode of consciousness which each is. The word 'image' can indicate only the relation of the consciousness to the object. The fact is that the expression 'mental image' is confusing. It would be better to dispense with the special noun 'image', and speak instead of 'imaginative consciousness' of a chair, of Peter, etc. In practice, however, the word has to stay because of its long, though dishonourable, history. When Sartre goes on to specify what exactly that mode of consciousness is which is called imagining, there is a certain disastrous ambiguity in his words. He says that imagining consists of three elements: there is an act, an object, and a content representative of an object. The act is the act of thinking of the object; the object is the chair, or Alice in Wonderland, or whatever we are thinking of; the content is *something* which is present to the mind as an object of attention, but which is merely an *analogical representation* of the thing thought of. We feel as if the object of consciousness really had the properties of the chair or whatever it is. But in fact only the chair has these properties. The content of our mind *represents* the properties by analogy, and in its own way. So far we do not seem to have advanced very far. The image, it is true, has been thrown out as a *thing*; but a mysterious representative object seems to have been let back in its place.

The nature of this object of consciousness, and the way in which it represents, are discussed by Sartre under the heading of the probable or speculative. This is the most interesting and debatable part of the book. The representation of this mental content consists in three things: there is imaginative knowledge—that is to say, when one imagines something one imagines it in all its concrete detail; there is *affectivity*, or the effect which the imagining may have upon our emotions—as when, for instance, the image of a hated object carries with it the appropriate feelings; and, thirdly, there are certain superficial and unimportant kinaesthetic sensations which accompany the image, but here will not be further discussed. These, then, are said by

Sartre to be the components of the representational composition of the image, which consists also of act and object.
But what is it exactly that does the representing? What is it
which has, for instance, spatial properties, not exactly, but
by analogy? What is it which has the required effect upon
our emotions? These questions may be thought to be put in
a tendentious form, and to reintroduce the very mental
entity which Sartre is trying so hard to get rid of. But, all
the same, there is considerable ambiguity in his answer.
On the whole, he seems to be saying this: when we conceive
of Peter in an imaginative, as opposed to a perceptual, way,
and this conceiving is the *act*, there is something which
comes into existence, and is a mental content. Peter is the
object of the act; but besides Peter himself there is a
temporary phantom object, which represents him by analogy, which is *sui generis*, and which falls into nothingness
immediately it has come into existence. He says: 'An
image, like all psychic syntheses, is something different
from, and more than, the sum of its elements. What counts
here is the new meaning that penetrates the whole. I want
to be with Peter. I want to believe he is here. My whole
consciousness is directed to him, it is fascinated in some
way. And this spontaneity, this intention towards Peter,
causes to flash forth this new phenomenon, which is
comparable to nothing else, the consciousness of the image.
This consciousness represents a mental form. When consciousness assumes this form it gives rise, for a moment, to
a stable appearance; then the form, carried by the current,
disintegrates and vanishes.' So there *are* objects of imagination; and they will be of the same kind whether what I am
thinking of is Peter, who exists though elsewhere, or a
golden mountain, which has no existence anywhere. The
objects of imagination are unique. But all of them have this
in common, that, though they are 'stable appearances',
they are *nothing*. Thus the act of imagination is essentially
this: a grasping of *nothing*, a projecting and positing of
what is not, *le néant*.
This essential characteristic leads us back once again to

the other kind of Cartesianism, namely to our awareness of freedom. For freedom consists, as we saw, in the power which we have to deny and to reject, and also to project what is not the case. This, Sartre insisted, against Descartes, was the essential creative freedom which men have. And now it turns out to be this very same power of envisaging what is *not* the case which makes us capable of framing images; that is, of exercising imagination at all. 'For consciousness to be able to imagine, it must be able, by its own efforts, to withdraw from the world. In a word, it must be free.' Thus the essential nothingness of the imagined object is what distinguishes it from the object of perception. And the two modes of consciousness, perception and imagination, which are alike in other respects, are distinguished from one another by this fact, that imagination necessarily carries with it the concept of freedom in this very special sense.

Here for the first time we are confronted by a wholly characteristic Sartrean argument. After all, it might be objected, there is nothing very surprising in the conclusion that imagination differs from perception in that the objects of the latter are real while those of the former are not. Is this, indeed, anything more than a necessary starting point? If we did not understand this much about them how could we even begin an enquiry into the essence of imagination? There would be some justice in this observation. The whole elaborate argument, started in the exposition of Descartes, and worked out in the course of two books on the imagination, has led in the end only to a staggering platitude—that imaginary objects are unreal. But to say this would be unduly unsympathetic, and unduly simple. Imagination has been *re*defined. All the definitions which made it a kind of thinking, or a kind of peering at mental entities called images, have been rejected. It has been redefined as the mode of consciousness of an object, whether an existent or non-existent object, which entails the bringing into fleeting existence of an appearance which fades at once to nothingness. And this is significant for

Sartre, just because he has already more than half formed the concept of human nature which is expounded in *Being and Nothingness*, and which turns essentially on the possibility of projecting what is not the case. This is what is here included in the definition. Thus, it is not so much the definition itself which we ought to consider, as the manner in which it coheres with, and confirms, other definitions. Man's ability to imagine things, which, of course, was never in doubt, is now shown to be connected, in its essence, with his ability to choose. And this is something which, whether we think it true or false, reasonable or unreasonable, is certainly not a mere platitude.

Sartre goes on to elaborate other differences between the objects of perception and those of imagination, besides this glaringly obvious one. For instance, there is an essential poverty which he ascribes to objects conceived imaginatively, by contrast with those perceived. This poverty may in fact be said to be just another aspect of the obvious distinction between the real and the unreal. For it consists in the failure of imagined objects to be properly related to other things in the world, and their failure to conform, as real things do, to laws of individuation and identity. Once again we may be inclined to complain that there is nothing here which is not perfectly obvious to anyone who knows what the words 'real' and 'imaginary' mean. Why treat these facts as great discoveries? But here the point of the distinctions is to be found in the manner in which they were arrived at. For they are the outcome of a serious attempt to see what imagining is actually like, and what features we can actually discern in the things we imagine if we try to clear our minds of presuppositions and assumptions about the world. The results may seem self-evident, but they have been reached by a version of the phenomenologists' *epoche*. What we have here is a description of what imagining is. And this description is to be taken as an addition, in a different mode, to what we may call the general metaphysical conclusion already arrived at—namely, that man is essentially capable of freely envisaging *le néant*, and that it is in this freedom that his power to imagine things consists.

Images and imagining, then, are thought to be differentiated from other kinds of consciousness of things by certain discernible features which they possess, and which we can realize if we think carefully enough. There is no difficulty, Sartre says, in distinguishing concepts or thoughts on the one hand from images on the other. For neither concepts nor images exist as *things* at all; but there are two discernibly different ways in which the concept of something can appear to us—as a pure thought on the reflective level, or as an image on the non-reflective level. And we pass perpetually from one way of thinking to the other. Thinking is the genus, and imaging a species of this genus, which we can recognize by perceptible features.

But Sartre has to admit that the possibility of hallucination raises some doubts about his theory. For, so far, everything he has said suggests that imaging or having images is immediately recognizable as such by the person who does it, and at the time that he does it. I cannot fail to know whether I am perceiving something or imagining it; nor whether I am merely intellectually *thinking* of something or imagining it, because of the nature of the actual process of imagining. This would suggest that I can never be deceived into supposing that I am perceiving when really I am only imagining. And yet we all believe that such deception is sometimes possible.

Sartre admits, then, that this might seem to be a stumbling block for his theory; but he thinks that the questions we ask about hallucination should be re-phrased. We should not ask 'How do we come to mistake an image for a perception?' but 'How do we come to feel passive before an image?' For Sartre maintains that in fact, in hallucinatory experience, the image *is* recognized as such, only there is another feeling present as well, namely the feeling that the patient cannot help having the image, though he knows in a way that it is made by himself. Moreover, the presence of the image coincides with a sudden absence of proper awareness of the outside world.

It seems to me that there is a great deal to be said for this kind of account of hallucinations. A theory very like it is to be found in the works of Brentano, who was inclined to think that even on the first occasion of suffering an hallucination the patient knew that it was not a true perception, and so, for instance, he went to consult a doctor; but the patient could describe the experience in none but perceptual terms, adding only the kind of descriptive features that we should expect of an image—for instance, that it failed to relate to the rest of his perceptual experience. It may be, however, that there are other kinds of hallucinatory experience which will not fit into this account. But, for what it is worth, we should notice that Sartre is one of the only philosophers who discuss this subject who is known to have suffered from hallucinations himself. Simone de Beauvoir describes an occasion when she and Sartre spent the whole night walking about in Paris, and she says that afterwards Sartre told her that he had been followed all night by a lobster. And at this time he often suffered from the same kind of hallucination. However that may be, by means of this account of hallucination Sartre has saved his definition of imagination as that which can be immediately recognized to be different both from perception and from intellectual thought, even in this difficult case.

He does not say very much about dreams, but it is probable that he would be inclined to treat them in the same way as hallucinations—as an awareness of an object combined with, in this case, a total unawareness of the rest of the perceptible world. They would therefore be intrinsically different from other kinds of awareness of objects, but would still fall under the genus of thought, as all imagining does. This seems to be an obviously right approach to the problem of what dreams are like, and how they are distinguished from waking experiences. The fact that *at the time* we are not in a position to say 'I am dreaming' in the way we can say 'I am thinking' need not trick us into believing that there is no difference between dreams and waking experience. Here, as elsewhere in his treatment of the imagination, Sartre is strongly, and it seems rightly, opposed to Cartesianism; indeed, the whole of his treatment of the imagination may be taken as a counterblast to the well-known dictum of Descartes that 'there are no certain indications by which we may clearly distinguish wakefulness from sleep'.

The whole of the discussion of the imagination, a great deal of which has been entirely left out of my account, is thus a deduction from and an elaboration of the doctrines of Husserl. But it is also an integral part of that whole systematic philosophy of human nature which is fully developed in *Being and Nothingness*. For there man's capacity both to perceive the world and to act upon it is dependent on his freedom, and this freedom expresses itself in his ability to see what things are *not*, to envisage possibilities, and to accept or reject what has been envisaged. This capacity has so far been shown, if that is the right word, to be identical with man's capacity to imagine.

(b) *The emotions*

The second preliminary to *Being and Nothingness*, the discussion of the emotions, is yet more closely connected with human actions upon the world. Here we have what is, admittedly, only a sketch of a theory, but one which it is essential to examine if we are to understand the psychological presuppositions of Sartre's philosophy as a whole.

The *Sketch for a Theory of the Emotions* was published in 1939. In it Sartre follows exactly the same procedure as we saw him using in *The Imagination*. He first expounds and criticizes various theories which he thinks mistaken, and then says that he regards it as the task of a phenomenological account of emotion to correct these mistakes. The sketch which follows is a sketch of the phenomenology of emotion. This, incidentally, is a subject, like that of the imagination, which lies on the borderline between psychology and philosophy, being in different ways relevant to both. But it would be exceedingly well worth while for philosophers to investigate it more than they do. It has been somewhat neglected compared with the well-trodden ground of imagery, perhaps because it was more cursorily dealt with by seventeenth- and eighteenth-century philosophers, and doubtless also because it is less clearly relevant to epistemology. However, it has some connexion with the latter subject, especially for Sartre, as we shall see.

In order to understand the theory which he proposes it is perhaps necessary, however briefly, to take a look at the theories which he rejects. He starts with the theory held by William James, and known as the Peripheric theory, according to which emotion is the consciousness of physiological disturbance. According to this theory to speak of an emotion *causing* physical symptoms in the person who feels it is to put the cart before the horse. Sadness does not cause tears; on the contrary, James prefers paradoxically to say that the tears, the physiological disturbance, cause the sadness, which is the consciousness of the disturbance. This view has been rightly criticized by Sartre, and by others, on the ground that it is totally inadequate for distinguishing one emotion from another. There are far fewer recognizable kinds of physiological disturbance than there are kinds of emotion, and no account is offered of the multiplicity, or of the subtlety, of our emotional responses to things. In any case, Sartre says, the theory fails to account for the plain fact that our emotional life is not, as it would suggest, entirely chaotic. It is to some extent organized, and to some extent meaningful. 'Emotion presents itself to us as a certain relation between our psychological being and the world.'

Janet's theory is treated more sympathetically by Sartre. Janet, himself critical of James for leaving out the psychological component of emotion, treats emotion as a twofold kind of behaviour, both mental and physical. He attempts to account for both elements, by defining emotion as *the behaviour of defeat*. In the example discussed in Sartre's *Sketch* a girl breaks down in tears because the alternative, that of discussing her case with her doctor, is too difficult for her: weeping is an easier substitute. Sartre argues

B

against this view that, while it introduces a notion of finality or purposiveness which must indeed be included in the definition of emotion, it introduces it without any justification. Janet, he argues, has no business to make use of the concept of finality, since he does not introduce any kind of consciousness or awareness, which alone could bring the concept of purpose into his definition. Janet fails, that is to say, to show that the mental element in emotion, as he describes it, is such as to be capable of supporting the idea of a purpose. The mental element here, as in the peripheric theory, is not sufficiently cognitive. If behaviour is to be purposive it must have an end actually *in view*.

Incidentally, Sartre's criticism here of Janet is highly characteristic of his most favoured style, the anecdotal. He takes up the story of the girl and her doctor, and presents it in a different light. According to Sartre, she weeps, not because she finds she cannot talk to him, but *in order that she shall not have to talk to him*, although she half wants to. And thus she is presented as self-deceiving, as behaving 'in bad faith', in a manner which has an important place in Sartre's final account of human nature in *Being and Nothingness*, and which is richly illustrated there. The reason offered for preferring this account of the girl's behaviour is that it quite explicitly employs the concept of purpose by treating emotions as an 'organized pattern of means directed towards an end'.

Next, Sartre examines Dembo's theory. This, in his view, comes even nearer to being a true account of the emotions. According to this theory, anger, for instance, is an alternative way out of a difficulty, used when all other ways have been blocked. It is, as are all the other emotions, the resort of frustration. But this is an essentially inferior way out; it is a means which we adopt towards an end, but we adopt it with an inferior part of ourselves. We become less self-critical in moments of frustration, and we are therefore prepared to make use of means which normally we should reject. This account, Sartre says, is perfect so far as it goes, but it is still not sufficient. For there can be no change from one, superior, form of behaviour to another, inferior, form, without consciousness. One form cannot take over from another unless it 'presents itself clearly as the alternative form'. It is necessary therefore to have recourse explicitly to the consciousness, as soon as it is realized that an account of emotion must describe a certain relation between the subject and the world outside him.

Thus James, Janet, and Dembo are represented by Sartre as moving, through increasingly adequate theories, towards the conclusion that emotion can be described only in cognitive terms—in terms, that is, of consciousness. Sartre's own view of what is meant by consciousness becomes clearer in the course of his next critical discussion, which is of the psycho-analytic theory of emotion, or the theory of the unconscious. Here, as often in *Being and Nothingness*, Sartre is explicit concerned to substitute his own theory for that of Freud. To accept the doctrine of the unconscious is, he says, to reject Cartesianism. And this, as we have seen already, means rejecting the concept of the pre-reflective 'cogito'. In this essay more clearly than elsewhere he comes out with the view that self-consciousness, at least in the sense of non-reflective awareness accompanying all that we think or do or intend to do, must *always* be present in human beings. 'Cartesianism' is simply used as the name of the view that consciousness is always aware of itself. And this has the consequence that Freudianism must be false, since there can be no such thing as an active but unconscious part of the human mind.

Within the framework, then, of his general rejection of Freudianism, Sartre here has certain specific points to make against the psycho-analytic theory of the emotions. What, he asks, can properly count as an explanation of conscious phenomena? The explanation of any thought or dream or feeling of which we may be aware must be sought, he says, not outside consciousness, but within it, for instance in some purpose framed by the same mind, or some object deliberately *meant* by it. Consciousness cannot be regarded

just as an ordinary *thing*, like a stone or a pond. It is
essentially intentional; it is always directed on to something,
and *means* that thing. So an emotion which is part of my
mental life, and a part of consciousness, means something
by being directed towards some object of its own. It can
be explained only in terms of this object, just as my words
can be explained only by reference to what they signify,
what I mean by them, and not by any causal or inductively
established relation which may be found experimentally to
hold between my utterance and the external world. Words,
that is, are not like stones and ponds either.

Now the psycho-analytic theory of the emotions has this
advantage, that it sees that emotions signify something
other than themselves. Indeed, according to Sartre, this
theory rests on the assumption that *every* state of consciousness signifies something other than itself. But the psycho-
analysts commit the mistake of cutting off what is symbolized entirely from that which symbolizes it. They hold,
that is to say, that in order to find out the signification
of any of my mental experiences it is no good my asking
myself what it means, or trying to understand it with
reference to any other part of my conscious mental life.
They think that the only method available for understanding what is meant by a certain feeling, for instance, or
a certain image, is an inductive method. According to the
theory it is possible externally to observe a certain relation
between a feeling and some past event in the life of the
person who experiences it; and this past event is then said
to be what is signified by the feeling. But this method of
interpretation would be like the method of someone who,
in total ignorance of a language, tried to work out some
observable causal, or at least regular, connexion between,
for instance, utterances by the users of the language of the
sound 'table' and some other observable phenomenon in
the world. It would be no good asking the user of the word
what he meant, since you would not understand his reply.
So the only method left, and it is true that it would be
hopelessly unsatisfactory, would be to watch what seemed

to be going on when he said the word 'table'. Sartre says: 'A theory of emotion which rightly insists on the signifying character of emotional facts should seek what is signified *in the consciousness itself.*' Not to do this constitutes the rejection of Cartesianism. It is impossible to treat the relation of signifying to thing signified as a *causal* or inductively established relation. This amounts, then, to an argument against the unconscious. For, of course, the Freudian theorist would not wish to say that there was *no* regular connexion between the felt emotion and what it stood for, but only that the patient who experiences the emotion does not understand what the connexion is, because he has made the connexion unconsciously.

So Sartre finally comes to his own account of the emotions; and, as we should now expect, he wants to say both that emotions are intentional, like all other mental events, and also that we deliberately direct our mind upon an object, and know, or can be made to recognize, what we are up to in feeling the emotion that we do. What the emotion signifies is available to us, because we adopt the emotion consciously, as a means to an end. However, Sartre is prepared to allow that it is just this which the psycho-analysts and others might wish to deny. For, they may argue, we are *not* in fact aware of what we are up to in feeling as we do in particular situations. Moreover, very often, far from deliberately adopting a certain way of feeling, we struggle to suppress an emotion which 'invades us in spite of ourselves'. It is to the solution of this difficulty—a difficulty, Sartre thinks, for Cartesianism—that the phenomenological theory of the emotions must address itself.

Emotional consciousness is, he says, at first at least, unreflective. That is, it is what he calls 'basic thetic consciousness of an object'. It may be, and generally is, accompanied by unreflective self-consciousness (the 'pre-reflective cogito'), which entails, as we have seen, an awareness of myself *being* aware of an object. But this is as far into reflectiveness as emotional consciousness need go.

The main point to grasp is that, just as much as perception itself, which is a matter of unreflective consciousness, emotion is a certain way of apprehending the world. There is an analogy, then, between emotion and perception. An even closer analogy may be found between emotion and *action*. We operate upon the world, do things in it, and change it, as a result of seeing it in a certain light. The operations we perform are often performed at the pre-reflective level; that is to say, we are aware of the world of objects, and we are aware all the time of ourselves acting, but we do not stop to try to make *ourselves* an object of thought in a fully reflective way. We think, as far as we do think, about the world. This thought is accompanied by a vague awareness of ourselves, but that is all. Now as soon as we think of *doing* things in the world rather than merely contemplating it, we necessarily see the world as 'difficult'. This difficulty is apprehended as one of the properties of the objects which we see; for instance, I see a hill, and see at once that it is steep, which is a difficulty for me if I mean to climb it. We see the world as making certain demands on us. So it is that one cannot fully distinguish between merely perceiving the world and acting on it. In perception we see things-to-be-done. This is simply a fact about human beings. We make a kind of map of the world for ourselves, what Sartre calls a *hodological* map, charting out the paths by which we have to reach our various goals; and in the light of this map we see the world as if it were an artefact of our own.

But there are blocks and difficulties as well as routes, and when these become too great for us we pretend that we can get what we want by magic instead of by proper natural means. Sartre says: 'We can now conceive what an emotion is. It is a transformation of the world. When the paths before us become too difficult, or when we cannot see our way, we can no longer put up with so exacting and difficult a world. All ways are barred and nevertheless we must act. So then we try to change the world; that is, to live in it as though the relations between things and their potentialities

were not governed by deterministic processes but by magic....
Our effort is not conscious of what it is, for then it would
be an object of reflection. It is, above all, an apprehension
of new relationships and new demands. The apprehension
of the object being impossible or giving rise to an unbearable tension, the consciousness apprehends it, or tries to
apprehend it, otherwise. That is, tries to transform itself
in order to transform the object.' Under stress, then, one
sees the world in a new light, and seeks to transform the
world, though ineffectively.

Sartre illustrates this by a somewhat absurd example: 'I
lift my hand to pluck a bunch of grapes. I cannot do so;
they are beyond my reach; so I shrug my shoulders,
muttering "They are too green", and go on my way. The
gestures, words, behaviour, are not to be taken at face
value. This little comedy that I play under the grapes,
thereby conferring the quality of being "too green" upon
them, serves as a substitute for the action I cannot complete.
They presented themselves first as "ready for gathering";
but this attractive quality soon becomes intolerable when
the potentiality cannot be actualized. The disagreeable
tension becomes, in turn, a motive for seeing another
quality in the grapes; their being "too green"; which will
resolve the conflict and put an end to the tension. Only I
cannot confer this quality upon the grapes chemically. So
I seize upon the tartness of grapes that are too green by
putting on the behaviour of disgust. I thus confer the
required quality upon the grapes magically. In this case
the comedy is only half sincere. But let the situation be more
critical; let the incantatory behaviour be maintained in all
seriousness, and there you have emotion.'

It must be admitted that this account fits best those
emotions which are, one way or another, distressing, such
as anger or despair. It is difficult to make it work as an
account of the agreeable emotions. But it seems intelligible
enough as, for example, an account of the feeling of horror
which we may experience on seeing a face at the window—
another of Sartre's examples. The concept of magic here

has a double role. We feel terror because we are seeing the world, not rationally as a set of means and ends, nor as a collection of tools which we may use, or methods which may be employed for this or that purpose, but as one 'non-utilizable' whole. That is to say, the object of terror acts upon us *immediately*, and we do not use the normal categories of the possible and the impossible. Rationally, we might calculate that the window is shut, that the man outside could not get in, and that if he did he would not harm us; but none of this enters into the horrific vision of the face. It is as if it were not separated from us by any space, nor by any other physical objects which would afford us protection. And since the face terrifies us as a magical object which is not bound by ordinary physical impossibility, we attempt to combat the danger by magic too; not, that is, by taking rational steps to achieve our aim, but by screaming or fainting to blot out the horror. Even running away when we are afraid, according to Sartre, is not something we do *in order to take shelter*. We do it, if we cannot annihilate ourselves by fainting, in order to render the object of terror non-existent by magic. 'The magical' is the name of one of the many fundamental ways we have of seeing the world in which we live. It is an inferior and more primitive way of seeing it than the way of seeing which is normal to us in our practical life. So emotion is a kind of relapse into an inferior mode of consciousness. 'Emotion arises when the world of the utilizable vanishes abruptly, and the world of magic appears in its place.'

If the general definition of emotion is that it is substitute-action according to inferior rules, the phenomenology of the emotions would analyse the particular emotions and show how this general description applied to each. This would be the empirical part of the theory. But Sartre says that the theory is also *a priori*, in that it starts from a concept of man as *a being in the world*, but a being of a certain describable kind and with certain describable potentialities. He views his task in propounding such a theory as partly descriptive and partly metaphysical. He is not concerned merely to define or describe emotion, but also to show that human beings are of such a kind that they *must* necessarily adopt the characteristic behaviour which he ascribes to them. Just as, in his treatment of the imagination, he aimed to show that man, being capable of freedom, was therefore also committed to imagining in the manner he described, so here he hopes to derive the description of the emotions from far more general facts about man, situated in the world in which he is surrounded *by things to be done*.

What we have learned specifically from the *Sketch* is that acting upon the world is a way of being aware of the world. There is no sharp distinction between doing things and seeing them in a certain light—as things *to be done*. And it is impossible to describe human beings without at the same time describing them as having some cognitive relation to the world. The central existentialist doctrine is that men are nothing but what they choose to become, their essence consists in what they choose to do. But it also consists in what they choose to *know*, the aspect under which they choose to see the world. Emotion arises when they choose to see it in a particular way, namely the magical. It is an essential part of human nature to be capable of this.

So it is that Cartesianism—or more properly phenomenology, which is based on the assumption that it is possible to describe human consciousness in general, but directly—leads to the description of the modes in which human beings are conscious of the world in which they are placed. Imagination and emotion are two essential modes of awareness of the world. In *Being and Nothingness*, which we are now in a position to examine, Sartre gives us his systematic description of man's place in the universe, to which these limited essays in description are essential preliminaries.

2

Nothingness

(1) Three modes of being

When we turn to *Being and Nothingness* we find ourselves
confronted by a very large, highly integrated system of
concepts, the purpose of which is mainly descriptive. It is
difficult, in trying to present an exposition of this book,
to decide at what point to break into the system. But at the
same time it does not very much matter where we begin,
since the concepts employed are genuinely interrelated, and
each must be understood in terms of the others. Perhaps the
fundamental distinction, to begin with, is that between
different *modes of being*. Of these there are three. We must
distinguish, Sartre holds, between Being-in-itself, Being-
for-self, and Being-for-others. (I shall not, incidentally, say
anything at all about the origins of these expressions or
their history in Hegelian and German idealist philosophy
in general. Sartre owes a very great deal to Hegel, and also
to Heidegger. But these philosophers are themselves so
exceedingly obscure that more would be lost than gained
in trying to trace the debts and the corruptions, the like-
nesses and differences, which are, however, certainly there
to be traced by anyone who has the patience to undertake
it.)

These are the three modes of existence, and the aim of
the whole book can be said to be to explain the relation of
the first to the second, of Being-in-itself to Being-for-
itself; and this is done partly by means of the third mode,
Being-for-others. Being-for-itself is identical with conscious
being. Human beings are often referred to as 'the For-

itself'. Consciousness, then, is what is in fact being defined in the definition of the For-itself, the discussion of which occupies Part II of *Being and Nothingness*.

(2) *The gap within consciousness*

The essential characteristic of the For-itself is that it is a lack. It needs something to complete it. This lack is described in a whole number of different ways by Sartre. He says that consciousness is a vacancy or an emptiness. He says that it essentially consists in a gap—a gap, that is, between thought and the object of thought. This is by now familiar to us. Consciousness, according to the pheno-menological 'Cartesianism', has to be intentional; that is to say, it has to have an object. And at the same time as it is aware of an object it is aware, as we have seen, of the fact that it *is* so aware. This is the 'pre-reflective cogito'. Thus consciousness knowingly places itself at a distance from its objects; it distinguishes between itself and that which it is the consciousness of. And the very making of this distinction creates a gap, or distance, between thought and its object.

This leads on to the next and most important character-istic of consciousness, which, once again, was contained in Sartre's version of Cartesianism. The gap between the thought and its object actually consists in the power which consciousness has of affirming or denying; of accepting what is true of its object, and also of inventing, and of thinking what is false or of rejecting it. Freedom, we saw, consisted in this ability to affirm or deny, and to imagine what was not the case; and this freedom turns out to be that which constitutes the gap between thought and object, which is the essence of consciousness. So at the very centre of the For-itself, right at the beginning, we discover both freedom and an emptiness. We shall return to this later.

In explaining what he means by the lack which is charac-teristic of consciousness Sartre makes use of the concept of the *possible*. He says: '[Consciousness] lacks something *for* something else . . . as the broken disc of the moon lacks that which would be necessary to complete it, and transform it into a full moon.' What is lacked by a conscious being is 'the coincidence of himself with himself'. That is to say, the For-itself seeks for the self-identity or the completeness which is the characteristic of a *different* mode of being, namely *Being-in-itself*: 'What I ceaselessly aim towards is myself, that which I am not, my own possibilities.' 'Human reality both is and is not its own possibilities.'

Sartre takes a certain amount of trouble to explain what he means by 'the possible', but nevertheless it is difficult to be quite sure what he means. He wishes to say that the possibilities of a thing actually *belong* to it, as properties. When we say that it may possibly rain we do not simply mean that we can conceive either of its raining or of its not raining, without logical contradiction. We mean more than this; we are referring, he says, to some actual feature of the clouds. 'The possible is a concrete property of already existing realities. In order for the rain to be possible there must be clouds in the sky.' But he does not wish to be thought, in saying this, to fall into an acceptance of Aristotelian 'potentialities'—an extra collection of properties existing in things, alongside their actualized properties. He insists that unless there were conscious beings in the world there would be no such thing as possibilities. The mere properties of physical objects, though they are necessary before we can talk of possibilities, are not by themselves sufficient to entitle us to do so. We need also to see the world as organized in a certain way—to bring to bear, for instance, our inductively acquired knowledge of the world, to judge what categories of things we are dealing with—before we can see something as possible. 'The possibility of being stopped by a fold in the cloth belongs neither to the billiard ball that rolls, nor to the cloth; it can arise only in the organization into a system, of the ball and the cloth, by a being which has a comprehension of possibles.' Thus to say of Being-for-itself or consciousness that it strives all the time towards its own possibilities is to say that it is self-aware; for without the awareness and the organizing faculty of a mind thinking of possibilities there would be no possibilities to strive towards.

So once again we are confronted by the quasi-Cartesian conclusion that consciousness is always aware of itself in some vestigial manner. At the same time the comprehension of possibilities is, obviously, identical with the capacity for conceiving of what is not actual, what is not yet the case; so that the two essential characteristics of the For-itself come together once more under this heading.

Consciousness according to Sartre is always referring forward, away from a more momentary awareness of what is true now. Even if one tries to perform a phenomenologist's *epoche*, and to describe the immediately present content of consciousness, still one rushes ahead and is aware of future possibilities. Even in assigning names to things one is, in a sense, going forward into the future, and assuming something about how they will turn out. Sartre says: 'Consciousness of reading is not consciousness of reading this letter or this word or this sentence or even this paragraph; it is consciousness of reading this *book*, which refers me to all the pages still unread, to all the pages already read, which by definition detaches consciousness from itself. A consciousness which was conscious only of what it is would be obliged to spell out every word.' So the lack which is at the heart of consciousness is a lack of *completed possibilities*; and it must always remain unsatisfied as long as a being is conscious.

(3) Negation

We must now have a look at the concept of Negation, which also constitutes the gap which lies at the heart of Being-for-itself. Here, as so often, Sartre has taken over a crucial Hegelian concept. For negation was the mainspring of the Hegelian Dialectic. But at this stage Sartre makes no use of the dialectic itself. It is far from clear that he had understood Hegel; but it is unnecessary to trace back his own complex views to their still more complex sources. Negation forms the subject-matter of Part I of *Being and Nothingness*. It is defined in terms of a man's evident ability to ask questions. In considering this ability Sartre discovers that, necessarily, if he can ask a question he must be prepared for a negative reply to it. And even if he asks a question such as 'What is reality like?' the answer, if there is one, even if it is affirmative in form, will rule out other answers, and thus the notion of what reality is *not* like will be included.

It is frequently remarked that it does not make sense to assert that a thing *has* a certain property unless it also makes sense to say that there are other properties, ruled out by this one, which it does *not* possess. But Sartre says that the realization of the possibility of negation is a function not only of our judgments about the world, but of our attitudes *to* the world before we make any judgments whatever; for instance, the concept of negation enters into *expectation*, which may be pre-verbal, and is essentially such that it may be disappointed. In the same sort of way we may intuitively apprehend, he says, the absences of things as well as their presences. I inspect the carburettor of my car, and see that there is *nothing wrong with it*; I expect Pierre to be at the café, and I see immediately that he is *not there*.

It is worth quoting a rather long passage to illustrate the way in which Sartre thinks not only that we can apprehend negation, but that negation itself, as we apprehend it, has a certain recognizable quality of its own. The scene is the café where I expect Pierre to be:

> It is certain that the café in itself with its customers, tables, seats, mirrors and lights and its smoky atmosphere, filled with the clatter of cups and saucers, the sound of voices and feet, is a thing full of being. And any intuitions I may have about parts of it are pervaded by these smells sounds and colours, all of them phenomena that have a transphenomenal meaning. Similarly, the actual presence of Pierre in some place I do not know is also a fullness of being. It would seem

that we have found fullness everywhere. But we must observe that perception always implies the building up of a form upon a background. No object or group of objects is expressly designed to be organized into form or background: it all depends on how I direct my attention. When I go into this café to look for Pierre, there occurs a synthetic organization of all the objects in the café into background against which Pierre is given as about to appear. The organization of the café into background is a preliminary nihilization. Each element in the room, person, table, seat, tries to isolate itself and bring itself into relief against the background formed by all the other objects, then falls back into the non-differentiation of this background and dissolves into it. For the background is that which is seen only incidentally, which is given only marginal attention. Thus this preliminary nihilization of all the forms which appear and are then absorbed into the total sameness of the *background* is the essential condition of the appearance of the main form, which in this case is Pierre. And this nihilization is actually apparent to my intuition; I witness the successive disappearance of all the objects before my eyes, particularly the faces, which hold my attention for a moment (Is that Pierre?) then immediately disintegrate just because they 'are not' Pierre's face. But if I finally discovered Pierre, my intuition would be filled with a concrete element. I should suddenly be fascinated by his face, and the café would organize itself into an unobtrusive presence around him. But Pierre is not here. This does not mean to say that I discover his absence in some precise corner of the establishment: rather Pierre is absent from the *entire* café: his absence fixes the café in its state of evanescence, the café remains *as background* and continues to appear as an undifferentiated whole to the marginal attention which is all I give it. It slips further away and continues its process of nihilization. Only it changes into the background in the interests of *a particular* form; it carries this form everywhere just before it, it holds it out to me everywhere: and this form which constantly creeps between my eyes and the real solid objects in the café is itself a continual process of disappearance, Pierre standing out as nothing against the background formed by the nothingness of the café. So that what is apparent to the intuition is a fluttering movement of non-existence, the non-existence of the background whose nihilization calls for and demands the appearance of the form and the form itself—a non-existence gliding like no-thing over the surface of the background. The basis of the judgment 'Pierre isn't here' is therefore formed by the intuitive apprehension of a twofold nothingness: and indeed Pierre's absence implies an initial connexion between me and the café. There are countless people who have not the slightest connexion with this café because there was no real period of expectation to establish their absence: but I was expecting to see Pierre, and my expectation has caused his absence to *happen* just like any real event to do with this café: and now his absence is an objective fact—I have *discovered* it and it is as it were a synthetic connexion between Pierre and the room in which I am looking for him. The absence of Pierre *pervades* the café and is the condition of its organizing itself, by a process of nihilation, into background; whereas any judgments I might make afterwards to amuse myself such as 'Wellington isn't in the café, neither is Paul Valéry', etc., are pure abstractions, nothing more than applications of the principle of negation, devoid of reference, and they do not succeed in establishing a *real* connexion between this café, Wellington, or Valéry. The relationship '*is not*' is here simply a thought-relationship. This demonstrates that non-being does not attach itself to things as a result of a negative judgment. On the contrary, it is the negative judgment which is conditioned and maintained by non-being.

This long passage, which is highly characteristic (in more ways than one) of *Being and Nothingness*, is also of primary importance in establishing the basic facts which Sartre thinks are true of the world, and which he thinks can be established just by describing the manner in which they come to our attention. *What is not the case* is a real part of our experience, and can be recognized to be such if we think about it. Another way of saying this, which we may deplore but which Sartre does not object to, is to say that there is such a thing as non-being in the world. However, in order to explain non-being, as this long example shows, one needs to set the scene to include some person in the role of expectant observer. It is our expectations and presuppositions which produce such concepts as 'absence'. But, granted that this is so, we can *perceive* absence as clearly as we can perceive presence. There is no question, then, but that negation enters into our awareness of the world, and therefore into our awareness of ourselves, at a very early, pre-rational level. And all knowledge whatever involves negation to this extent, that the person who knows, knows that he is *not* the object of his knowledge. He identifies himself by reference to the multitudes of things which are *different from himself*.

But Sartre has still more to say about the origin of the concept of negation. The possibility of negation was first introduced by means of the question. And later in the discussion Sartre goes back to this. He says, in a somewhat mysterious passage, that for someone to be able to frame questions he must be in a sense free of causal determinism. If everything were determined so that in every conceivable case, given one event, the next could be predicted, there would be no such thing as a question. For a question does not produce its answer in the way that fire produces heat. Nor is it possible to predict on inductive grounds, from observation of the world, what answer will be forthcoming to a question even if it is a question which one asks oneself. Causation, the sequence of determined events, is nothing but bare existence. One event follows another in a regular order in which each event exists. Nothingness or non-being has no place here. So Sartre says: 'It is essential that the questioner have the permanent possibility of dissociating himself from the causal series which constitutes being and which can produce only being. . . . In so far as the questioner must be able to effect in relation to the questioned a kind of nihilating withdrawal, he is not subject to the causal order of the world; he detaches himself from Being.' Thus, in posing a question, a certain negative element is introduced into the world. In order to ask a question it must be possible for the questioner to dissociate himself from what he is asking the question about, and see it in a neutral uncommitted way. 'This disengagement is then, by definition, a human process. Man presents himself . . . as a being who causes Nothingness to arise in the world, inasmuch as he is affected with non-being to this end.'

I have laboured at length this introduction of the concept of nothingness, negation and non-being; partly because it is obscure and may represent a kind of argument, if such it is, with which not everyone feels at home; but partly because this concept lies at the foundation of the whole structure of *Being and Nothingness*. Every further description which is designed to assign to human beings their place in the universe, their characteristic modes of behaviour in the face of the world and of one another, is ultimately based upon this fact—that they, and they alone, bring nothingness into being and are capable of conceiving what is not so. And it would misrepresent the general shape of the book if it were thought that Sartre simply introduces this notion of nothingness without at least an attempt to show how it arises in man's relation to the world.

(4) Bad Faith

(a) *Anguish*

By the end of the first chapter of the book it emerges, somewhat confusedly perhaps, that there is, in addition to the fact of non-being which is brought into the world by conscious beings, a characteristic kind of human behaviour, possible only to free conscious beings, the existence of which confirms the facts already described. That is to say, the existence of this kind of behaviour serves as additional proof both that nothingness or non-being is brought into the world by conscious beings and that thus bringing it into the world is an essential feature of consciousness. The characteristic kind of behaviour is *Bad Faith*—Mauvaise Foi—to the description of which Sartre devotes a good deal of highly characteristic imaginative ingenuity.

Bad Faith is treated by him as both a very important and a completely familiar human trait. And it is true that, once one gets used to employing the concept, it is easy to see this peculiar kind of insincerity everywhere, half self-deceiving, half deliberate, the playing of parts in one's life. But it is worth remarking that Sartre does not ever prove that this kind of behaviour is important, nor that it explains anything about the people who practise it. He takes it for granted that it occurs, and also that it is undesirable.

In this early part of *Being and Nothingness*, then, he uses the existence of Bad Faith, which he treats as a self-evident fact, to prove the existence of the power to conceive non-existence with which he is primarily concerned. He goes in for what is a kind of transcendental proof, a form of argument which he uses over and over again in his writings: if human beings were not capable of conceiving what is not true there would be no such thing as Bad Faith. But there is such a thing as Bad Faith; therefore they are capable of conceiving what is not the case. He actually uses this Kantian form of argument in a very Kantian way, by asking the question '*How is Bad Faith possible?*' This question is very different from the question 'Is it possible?' or 'Does it occur?' It can be expanded to the form: 'Granted that Bad Faith does occur, what are the human characteristics which are the necessary conditions of it?' And, as we have seen, the answer is that the necessary condition for Bad Faith is the grasping of nothingness, which is identical with the freedom of consciousness.

We may perhaps be forgiven, however, if we approach the matter in a rather different way, and try to find out from Sartre what Bad Faith is. For it may well be that here, as elsewhere, we may wish to dissent, if not from all that he says, at least from his emphases. Basically, Bad Faith is an attempt to escape from the anguish which men suffer when they are brought face to face with their own freedom. Conscious beings are essentially free, not only to act as they choose, but to see the world under the headings and categories that they choose. We have seen how their freedom is involved even in their accepting the truth about things or in imagining things which are not true. It is also involved in their choice of ends, and their mapping out the world as a set of roads towards these ends. They are even free to adopt hopeless and useless kinds of behaviour in the face of their difficulties, if they want to. They are free to make use of the magical, in emotion. We shall return in a later chapter to the great philosophical problems which are raised by the ascription of such unbounded freedom to human beings. At the moment it is the effect upon human beings of the contemplation of this freedom that we are concerned with.

If one suddenly realized that one was responsible not only for what one did, but for what one felt, and how in general one saw things, one might indeed wilt under so vast a burden of responsibility. One is, after all, greatly comforted by the thought that some features of one's life are inevitable. One did not choose them; one may wish they were otherwise; but there is nothing whatever to be done about it, nor does one have to reproach oneself in the least for their being as they are. This is very different from the case where one has quite deliberately made a choice and where one may be tormented by the feeling that it would have been better to choose differently, that if things go wrong one must blame oneself, and not some fate, and that perhaps it is not too late to take steps to change things and to reverse one's choice. All this is familiar enough. It is therefore understandable that Sartre, who thinks we are responsible for everything, also thinks that the burden of responsibility is more than we can bear; and so we develop tricks and devices for evading it.

Of these tricks, irony, for instance, is one. We may always adopt an ironic tone, in an attempt to show that we are not really committed to the views we express. It would be too much of a responsibility to come right out into the open and say, for instance, that we believe in something or love it; and so we pretend that we are not committed, and leave a loophole by adopting an ironic tone. But a much more important device is that of Bad Faith, whereby we pretend that things are inevitable when they are not. One way or another, Bad Faith consists in pretending to ourselves and others that things could not be otherwise—that we are bound to our way of life, and that we could not escape it even if we wanted to. Most appeals to duty, most suggestions that one could not have done otherwise, even most of our strong beliefs (such as the belief that we *must* return hospitality, or get up in the morning, or be polite) are instances of Bad Faith, since in fact we *choose* to do all these things, and we *need* not do them.

Freedom is essentially nihilating, because it contains the possibility of answering 'no' to every suggestion of what I should do, and of rejecting every project for the future which I may form. Anguish comes when I realize that there is inevitably a gap, as we have seen, between myself now and my possibilities, which are, however, genuinely *my* possibilities. I choose between them, and whatever I choose makes me what I am. Conscious beings, Beings-for-themselves, have no fixed essences which determine how they shall behave from the moment they are made. They create their essences as they go along, by constantly choosing to fill up the gap between themselves and their futures in one way rather than in another. Here we have come upon the central doctrine of existentialism, which can be defined as the belief that, for human beings, existence precedes essence; there is no *essential* human nature, given in advance. Men are stuck down in the world, and they become whatever they choose to become by doing and feeling what they choose to do and feel.

Of course, Sartre does not suppose that one is liable to suffer anguish all, or even much, of the time. Normally I take it for granted that my trivial day-to-day actions lead in a certain unquestioned direction. The actions lead themselves on, and once embarked on an ordinary day, one thing leads to another without my having to stop to think of myself at all. It is only when I do think of my actions in relation to myself, reflectively, that I am liable to suffer anguish. Mostly, in acting, I am aware of myself only in the pre-reflective manner, as we have seen.

Sartre takes the example of writing a book. For a great deal of the time I just write the next word, the next sentence, trying to finish the sentence, or the page, I have started, setting myself finite tasks, and getting them done with only the traces of self-awareness. In order for me to suffer anguish about the book it is necessary, Sartre says, that 'the book should appear in its relation with me. On the one hand I must discover my essence as *what I have been*. (I have been "wanting to write this book", I have thought of it, I have believed that it would be interesting to write it, and I have become such that you can no longer understand me without taking into account the fact that this book *has been* my essential potentiality.) On the other hand, I must discover the nothingness which separates my freedom from this essence: (I *have been* "wanting to write" but *nothing*, not even what I have been, can compel me to write it.) Finally, I must discover the nothingness which separates me from what I shall be: (I discover that the permanent possibility of abandoning the book is the very condition of the possibility of writing it, and the very meaning of my freedom). I must apprehend my freedom precisely by setting up this book as my potential, in so far as my freedom is the possible destroyer, in the present and the future, of what I am. That is, I must place myself on the level of reflexion. As long as I remain on the level of action, the book-to-be-written is only the remote and presupposed meaning of the act which reveals my possibilities to me. The book is only the implication of the action; it is not made an object, and posited for itself; it is not "a matter for consideration"; it is conceived neither as necessary nor contingent. It is only the permanent remote meaning, in terms of which I can understand what I am writing in the present, and hence it is conceived as *being*; that is, only by positing the book as the existing substratum on which my present existing sentence depends can I confer a determined meaning upon my sentence. . . . We act before positing our possibilities, and these possibilities which are disclosed as realized, or in process of being realized, refer to reasons for acting which cannot be challenged without a special act of reflexion. The alarm which rings in the morning refers to the possibility of my going to work, which is *my* possibility. But to apprehend the summons of the alarm as a summons is to get up. Therefore the very act of getting up is reassuring, for it evades the question "is work *my* possibility?". Consequently, it does not put me in a position even to consider the possibility of quietism, of refusing to work, nor the possibility of refusing the world, nor the possibility of death. In short, in so far as perceiving the meaning of the ringing is already to be up at its summons; this perception guarantees me against the anguished intuition that it is *I* who confer on the alarm clock its exigency . . . I and I alone.'

In all sorts of ways one is normally reassured. One is engaged in a world, Sartre says, of values. And something has only to happen to oneself or one's friends for the values 'to spring up like partridges'; it is also true that one is constantly hedged about by duties, or by indignation, or a sense of outrage, or whatever the appropriate sentiment may be. We find ourselves in a world 'peopled by demands', in the very heart of projects; and we act without thinking. But when we *do* turn to reflection we discover freedom. And 'anguish is the reflective apprehension of freedom itself'.

(b) *Becoming thing-like*

There are two main kinds of Bad Faith, which Sartre illustrates by well-known examples, but which it is necessary to distinguish once again, since they arise out of the fundamental distinction between Being-in-itself and Being-for-others. The first pattern of Bad Faith is that in which, to protect himself against the recognition of his own freedom, a conscious being, a Being-for-itself, pretends to be a *thing*, a Being-in-itself, which therefore has no choice, but is managed by other people, or is just inert. In the second pattern a conscious being pretends to be nothing except a Being-for-others, that is, he acts out the role that people have assigned to him, and he sees himself as whatever it is that people want him to be. So his acts again seem to be determined by how *he is meant to be*. The first pattern is illustrated by Sartre with the example of a girl who has gone out with a man for the first time:

> She is perfectly well aware of the intentions that the man who is talking to her is harbouring. She knows that sooner or later she will have to make a decision. But she does not want to feel its urgency: she devotes all her attention to the elements of respect and discretion that her partner's attitude contains. She does not see his behaviour as an attempt to bring about what are called the 'preliminaries': that is, she does not want to see the possibility of temporal development which his conduct offers. She limits his conduct to what it is in the present, and she refuses to read any but their explicit meaning into the remarks addressed to her. If he says, 'I admire you very much,' she divests the sentence of its sexual undertones and attaches to the conversation and behaviour of her interlocutor immediate meanings which she sees as objective qualities. The man talking to her seems sincere and respectful in the same way that the table is round or square or the wallpaper blue or grey. And the qualities she thus attaches to the person she is listening to become

congealed in a thing-like permanence which is nothing
more than the projection into time of the strict present.
The fact is that she does not know what she wants.
She is profoundly conscious of the desire she arouses,
but crude naked desire would humiliate and disgust
her. Yet she would find no charm in respect that was
respect and nothing more. In order to be satisfied she
needs a sentiment that is directed entirely towards her
person, that is, towards her full freedom, a sentiment
that is a recognition of her freedom. But at the same
time this sentiment must be wholly desire, that is, it
must be directed towards her body as an object. So
this time she refuses to recognize desire for what it is.
She does not give it a name. She recognizes it only in
so far as it is sublimated into admiration, esteem and
respect, and is absorbed into the higher forms it
produces, to the point of appearing as no more than
a sort of warmth and fullness. But now he takes her
hand. This act on the part of her companion threatens
to change the situation, by requiring an immediate
decision. Leaving her hand in his amounts to commit-
ting herself to a flirtation. Taking it away means up-
setting the uneasy and unstable harmony which is the
whole charm of the moment. She must put off the
time of decision as long as possible. You know what
happens next: the woman leaves her hand where it is,
but *does not notice* that she has left it. She does not
notice, because she happens at that moment, quite by
chance, to be absorbed in questions of the mind. She
carries her interlocutor off into the most elevated
regions of sentimental speculation. She talks about life,
her life; she discloses her essential nature: a person, a
conciousness. And meanwhile the separation of soul
and body is achieved. Her hand rests passively in the
hot hands of her companion, neither consenting nor
resisting: a thing.

Her hand, then, is a thing, quite separate from
herself, and she has disowned it and cannot be held

responsible for what happens to it. This is the first
pattern of Bad Faith, and it is, it must be said, instantly
recognizable and familiar.

(c) *Playing a part*

So is the second. Sartre illustrates this by the example of a
waiter in a café. He is observed by Sartre to be plainly
acting a part—manifestly playing at something. When the
question what is he playing is raised:

> You don't have to watch him long to find out: he
> is playing *at being* a waiter. There is nothing surprising
> about this. Play is a means of localizing and investi-
> gating. A child plays with his body in order to explore
> it, to make an inventory of it: the waiter plays with his
> situation in life in order to *realize it*. The obligation to
> do this is the same as is imposed on all business men.
> Their status is entirely one of show, and the public
> requires them to realize it as show. There is the grocer's
> dance, the tailor's, the auctioneer's, by means of which
> they try to persuade their customers that they are
> grocers, tailors and auctioneers and nothing more.
> A grocer who indulges in day-dreams is offensive to
> the customer because he is no longer wholly a grocer.
> Courtesy requires him to contain himself within his
> function as a grocer, like the soldier at attention who
> makes himself into a soldier-thing, by his direct but
> unseeing gaze which is no longer even intended to see,
> since it is the regulation and not the interest of the
> moment which determines the point on which his eye
> should rest. We take ample precautions to confine a
> man to what he is; it is as if we lived in continual fear
> that he would get out, overflow and suddenly elude
> his position. But at the same time the fact is that the
> waiter cannot be a waiter from within and immediately,
> as an inkwell *is* an inkwell, or a tumbler a tumbler.
> Not that he cannot form reflexive judgments or frame
> the concept of his situation. He knows perfectly well

what it 'means' . . . the obligation to get up at 5 a.m., to sweep in front of the shop before opening time, to put the percolator on, etc. He knows the rights it entails . . . the right to accept tips, union rights, etc. But all these concepts and judgments concern the transcendental: they deal with abstract possibilities, rights and duties belonging to a 'subject in law'. And it is precisely this subject that I *am supposed to be* and that I am not. Not that I don't want to be he, or that he is someone else. Rather there is no common measure between his being and mine. He is a 'representation' for other people and for myself, which means that I can be only *by representation*. But if I represent him to myself, then I am not he; I am separated from him like the object from the subject, separated by *nothing*. But this nothing isolates me from him; I cannot be he. I can only play at being he, that is, imagine that I am.

It will be clear from this quotation how the existence of Bad Faith is linked with the freedom of the imagination, which was itself defined, in *The Imagination*, as the power to conceive what was not the case. The movements and gestures of the waiter are *representative* of the waiter, in the way in which images may represent non-existent things by a kind of analogy. The waiter does not pretend to be a *thing*, as the girl does who treats her hand as a thing. He pretends to be *nothing but* what people label him—that is, a waiter.

Ought we to try to avoid Bad Faith? There is no doubt that Sartre, merely by so naming it, leads us to suppose that we should not practise it. And it is easy to agree that, in certain cases, we dislike and despise the kind of behaviour which consists in pretending that we *have* to do things which in fact we are plainly choosing to do because we want to. Moreover self-deception is both dislikable and pitiable; while clear-sightedness about what we are up to, and what we can and cannot choose, is admirable. But if all conscious beings are necessarily separated from their future actions and their vision of themselves by a gap; if consciousness actually consists in the presence of this emptiness which has to be filled by free thoughts and choices, then plainly we cannot avoid Bad Faith altogether. We may aspire to be whatever we are completely, but we can never achieve this. We cannot become *massif*, like ink-wells, as long as we remain conscious. Nor can we become nothing but a typical such-and-such, seen through the eyes of other people. So we are, in a sense, aiming at the impossible. The best we can do is to recognize the freedom we have, and use it, knowing that this is what we are doing. If we value certain kinds of behaviour highly we may try to behave in this way; but we should recognize that it is we, and we alone, who have assigned this value to our ideal. To believe that a certain way of life is valuable *in itself*, independently of our thinking it so, is to fall into the 'spirit of seriousness'; and this is identical with Bad Faith. For it leads us once again into the belief that we *must* behave in this way rather than that, that we are really *bound* by our obligations and undertakings; whereas in truth we are fulfilling them because we want to, and because we choose to live in this way rather than that.

We shall return to the question of how Sartre thinks that we ought actually to behave in a later chapter. Such a question cannot be raised until we have tried to clarify the mode of being which he calls Being-for-others. It will also be necessary to examine his actual descriptions of the world; for it is a characteristic of Sartre that he finds nothing surprising in the supposition that one can say what the world is like *in general*. He is no more alarmed by the prospect of such an undertaking than were the pre-Socratic Greeks, who thought it reasonable to say that everything was really water, or fire. And what the world is like partly settles the question of how we ought to conduct ourselves in it. But let us first see, if we can, what has so far been constructed on the foundation of the 'nothingness' which conscious beings bring into the world.

(5) Summary

In a world which consists of *things* there is, as a fundamental and inexplicable fact, consciousness as well. Consciousness is aware both of objects around it, and also of itself. To be perceived or known by a conscious being is all that can happen to an object in the world, a Being-in-itself. Sartre speaks of the upsurge of consciousness in the world as 'the only possible adventure in the In-itself'. Knowing and being known is one of the fundamental relations which hold between the For-itself and the In-itself; and Sartre tries to show that this relation can exist only because of the nothingness at the centre of the For-itself. For knowledge entails that the object known is held at a distance from the person who knows it: he distinguishes the object from himself, and he thereby forms the judgment, 'I am *not* the object.' This distance at which the object is held is the gap or nothingness at the heart of the For-itself. The capacity for forming negative judgments is not distinguished by Sartre from the capacity to accept the true and reject the false, nor from the equally important correlative capacity to accept the false and reject the true. And this capacity is identical with human freedom. It is the defining characteristic of the For-itself, or consciousness. From it has been derived the human power to imagine, and to know, and to act.

Freedom is built into the notion of consciousness; and it means the ability to adopt an attitude to the world in which we find ourselves, to see it in this light or in that. It also means the ability to fill the gap within us as we choose. The gap is what separates us, and is recognized as separating us, from the world. It is what enables us to know things in the world, and it is also there to be filled by plans and projects and actions of our own. Sartre, like Kant, thinks that there is in the universe a fundamental distinction between natural objects, governed by causal laws, and free or 'dynamic' beings, governed by laws of their own making. But Sartre founds this distinction upon the capacity which dynamic beings bring with them into the world of conceiving things differently from how they are. Without the gap or vacancy within them, conscious beings would become unconscious Beings-in-themselves, wholly determined by being whatever they are. To speak of the 'essence' of a thing is to speak of it as necessarily being as it is, and behaving as it does behave. Conscious beings have no essences. Instead of an essential core they have nothing. Beings-in-themselves have no possibilities; or, rather, all their possibilities are realized at once at the moment of creation. From then on they behave as they were made to behave. (It is noticeable that Sartre tends to take, as examples of Beings-in-themselves, artefacts such as ink-wells and paper-knives. It is not so clear whether worms and fishes have essences or not; but in so far as their behaviour is in principle predictable, presumably they do, even if they have no function.) A conscious being, on the other hand, is aware of his own possibilities, of what he is not, or is not yet. So it comes about that he can pretend to be whatever he likes, and try to be whatever he likes.

By the end of the second part of *Being and Nothingness* Sartre has reached this point in his metaphysical construction. The only kind of human behaviour he has discussed is the behaviour of Bad Faith, because this arises directly out of, and confirms the existence of, the nothingness in the centre of consciousness. He has described the situation of Beings-for-themselves, placed in a world of Beings-in-themselves and, in knowing them, perpetually feeling separated from them. He is now in a position to go on, in the third part of the book, to describe the relation of conscious beings to one another. The third part is entitled *Beings-for-others*, and without the definition of this, the account of existence in the world must remain incomplete.

3

Being-for-others

Sartre has described how, in Bad Faith, we aim to evade
our responsibilities by pretending to be *massif*, like Beings-
in-themselves; and how we do this either by treating our
bodies as things with an existence of their own (as one
might decide one day that at last one was ill, and one's body
was just a thing to be taken to hospital, cut up and looked
after by somebody else); or by treating ourselves as wholly
determined in our behaviour by the view which others take
of us. If I am thought by others to be a waiter, and labelled
as such, then this is the role I may decide to play.

Sartre's most extended treatment of this last kind of Bad
Faith is to be found not in *Being and Nothingness*, but in
his treatment of the novelist and playwright Jean Genet
in a book which forms a bridge between Sartre's philosophy
and his sociology. Genet was sent from an orphanage to
foster-parents, where he started to steal. When he was
discovered he was labelled a thief; and as soon as he heard
this said of him he decided that he must be what he was said
to be. Thereafter he devoted himself to a life of crime, and
was continually in and out of prison. The end of the story
was his own salvation of himself through literature. But
he was able to save himself only because he realized that he
had deliberately chosen to live as he had lived, just in order
to play out the part which society had selected for him. This,
then, is *one* of the effects which other people may have upon us.

But the notion of the relations of Beings-for-themselves
to one another is fully explored in the third part of *Being
and Nothingness*, and this is by far the richest and the most
extraordinary part of the whole book. Quotation cannot
really convey the inventiveness and the detail of this part.

It has been described as the only contribution to porno-graphic philosophy; and though this is misleading, there is at any rate more drama in this part of the book than one might expect in a work of metaphysics. Moreover, Sartre seems to me to be in fact more successful here than he always is in his novels at conveying a view of life—at conveying his impression, that is, of what people are actually like—though this is done in entirely general terms, helped out from time to time by his somewhat anecdotal examples.

(1) Awareness of other people

Being-for-others is defined in two related ways. First, I am aware of my own bodily existence as something which is known to other people. Secondly I am aware of the bodies of other people, and thence of their existence in the world. At the end of Part II Sartre says: 'What I know is the body of another, and the essential facts which *I know* concerning my own body come from the way in which others see it. Thus the nature of my body refers me to the existence of others and my Being-for-others.' And he goes on to say: 'If I want to describe in an exhaustive manner the relation of Man to Being, I must now attempt the study of this new structure of my being—the For-others. Within one and the same upsurge, the being of human reality must be for-itself-for-others.' Thus, it is immediately clear that for Sartre there is no such thing as the old philosophical problem known as 'the problem of other minds'. For this problem arose from the supposed fact that my awareness of the outside world was based on my knowledge of my own sensations and impressions. Of these I was supposed to be completely sure. But my impressions gave me no sign that other human beings were in any way different from other objects in the world, since I could be aware only of their outsides, not of their consciousness, nor of their sensations. Why then did I assume that they too were conscious, capable of thought and feeling? This was the problem.

And, roughly speaking, the traditional answer was that I argued to the existence of other minds by an analogy with my own case.

For Sartre, however, the problem cannot arise in this form. For the contention which he seeks to prove in the third part is that, at one and the same time as I am aware of myself, I necessarily become aware that other people exist and are observing me. If I were not aware of this fact I should be only partially conscious of myself. I might be conscious of my plans and thoughts, but I could not be conscious of myself—of my body—putting these plans and thoughts into practice. Awareness of myself as acting is identical with awareness of myself as an object—that is, as a possible or actual object of perception to another person. Thus our knowledge that other people exist, and are conscious, is part and parcel of our own awareness of ourselves.

Even if we confine our attention to an introspective account of our own consciousness we come upon elements in the description of it which entail that we exist for others and not merely for ourselves. Reflective self-awareness—that is to say, the realization that I am an object of attention for myself—cannot be wholly separated from knowledge that I am an object of attention for others. As an example to illustrate this point Sartre uses the concept of shame, which in fact he is to use again later in this part. Shame is something of which we are aware on introspection; it *of* also intentional—'it is the shameful apprehension *is* something, and this something is *me*'. And yet shame is not only, or primarily, a phenomenon of introspection, because in order to feel ashamed it is necessary to be aware of someone besides oneself. 'I have just made an awkward or vulgar gesture. This gesture clings to me; I neither judge it nor blame it. I simply live it. I realize it in the mode for-itself. But now suddenly I raise my head. Somebody was there and had seen me. Suddenly I realize the vulgarity of my gesture, and I am ashamed. . . . In the field of my reflection I can never meet with anything but my

C

own consciousness. But the Other is the indispensable mediator between myself and me. I am ashamed of myself as I appear to the Other. By the mere appearance of the Other, I am put in the position of passing judgment on myself as on an object, for it is as an object that I appear to the Other. Yet this object which has appeared to the Other is not an empty image in the mind of another. Such an image in fact would be imputable wholly to the Other and so could not "touch" me. I could feel irritation or anger before it, as before a bad portrait of myself which gives to my expression an ugliness or a baseness which I do not have, but I could not be touched to the quick. Shame is by nature *recognition*. I recognize that I am as the Other sees me.' There is no question, then, of comparing my view of myself as revealed to introspection with the Other's view of me. One cannot hold up one's Being-for-itself and compare it with one's Being-for-others. The recognition that I am as he sees me is immediate. 'Shame is an immediate shudder which runs through me from head to foot without any discursive preparation.'

But in any case comparison would be impossible. For myself, I am an object seen without distance or perspective; and this object cannot be compared with the Being-in-itself or thing-at-a-distance which I am for the Other. Moreover, 'no one can be vulgar all alone'. That is to say, there are certain predicates which I can apply to myself, which could not have any application to my Being-for-itself. Shame is shame of oneself *before* the Other. My Being-for-myself and my Being-for-others are essentially linked together by means of Being-in-itself. For this is what I have, in a way, in the eyes of other people. I am, after all, a physical object in the world, describable up to a point, and manageable up to a point by others, just as other physical objects are. The duality of mind and body, of physical thing and mental thing, is essential to human beings and determines their behaviour in many ways. For other people I am, at first and immediately, a Being-in-itself. For myself I am, naturally, a Being-for-itself. And together

these two modes of being combine to define the third
mode—Being-for-others.

(2) Historical account

(a) Epistemological

In working towards his full account of this mode of being,
Sartre, as usual, examines the theories of various other
philosophers. This examination is, as usual, interesting and
illuminating on its own account. It also serves to emphasize
an important difference between the Sartrean theory and
most, at least, of the others. The problem, as we saw, was
traditionally posed in the form: 'How do *I know* that there
are other minds than my own?' But Sartre asks rather:
'What is the fundamental relation that holds between one
person and another?' To this question, the epistemological
answer in terms of our *knowledge* of other minds is only a
preliminary part. Let us take a brief look at Sartre's
comments on previous theories.

First of all he considers Solipsism. Even realists, he says,
who claim to take the existence of others as certain, are
really treating other people's existence in the same way as
idealists. They really think that of other people it is true
that *to be is to be perceived*. 'Thus by a curious reversal the
realist, because he has posited the reality of the outside
world, is forced to return to idealism when he confronts the
existence of others. If the body is a real object really
acting on thinking substance, the Other becomes a pure
representation, whose *esse* is a simple *percipi*; that is, one
whose existence is measured by the knowledge we have of
it.' But this is unsatisfactory, and leads either to solipsism
or to a kind of dogmatic shuffling off of the problem.

Sartre concludes that if we persist in regarding the
question of the existence of others as merely a problem of
knowledge, we are necessarily reduced to the position of
thinking of ourselves as completely cut off from other
people, who may or may not have real existence apart
from our thought of them. For from whatever angle we

approach the question of knowing the mind of another we find that we cannot know it as we know our own mind. The only thing we can know as we know other things is the *appearances* of other people. If this is all we have, then we cannot construct the picture of a universe containing ourselves and others as equals, unless we introduce the further concept of an all-seeing eye which keeps me and other people perpetually in view, though we cannot keep one another in view. Sartre thinks of all such theories, which are primarily epistemological in the questions which they raise, as leading to something like a Lebnizian universe, peopled by independent 'windowless' monads, each complex in itself, but incapable of relations with others. The theory that all these monads were created by God only conceals the problem. God as creator is made to play the part of myself and of others indifferently. That is, he can know me as well as I know myself, and he can know other people as well as they know themselves, and he is introduced to conceal the impossibility of there being an interrelation of knowledge between me and others.

(b) *Husserl*

Sartre finds a recognition of this impossibility in some philosophers of the nineteenth and twentieth centuries. They therefore try, he says, to find something which is essential to consciousness itself, and which would yet necessarily reveal the existence of other people to me. But all the same, although there is this attempt in the theories of Husserl, Hegel, and Heidegger, which he goes on to consider, there is also the assumption that however the existence of other people is revealed to me, still the fundamental relation between myself and them is that of knowledge. Yet, as we should expect, Sartre finds much to admire in the theories of all these three philosophers.

According to Husserl, when I consider any object, a tree or a wall or a book, I always have the Other as part of the 'meaning' which belongs to the object I am considering. For each object that I consider appears to me as possessing relations to a consciousness other than my own. I cannot think of a tree as an object constituted just by its relations to *my* consciousness. If I thought of it in this way it would not be a real objective tree that I was thinking of. The existence of other people guarantees the objectivity of objects, and is therefore part of what constitutes my own consciousness, which is necessarily directed upon objects. Now this, according to Sartre, contains a germ of truth. But it overlooks what is crucial for Sartre's own description of the world, namely the fact that there are in the world numbers of different individual concrete persons, whom I recognize. The Other has the role, in Husserl's theory, of a category, an essential element out of which experience in general is built up for me. But the Other is here something quite *im*personal—a kind of abstract and general self-hood. Husserl gives us no clue how, in fact, we pass from this underlying general concept to the precise and particular concepts which we all of us have, in our actual experience, of the different people in the world.

(c) *Hegel*

Hegel's solution to the problem, contained in *The Phenomenology of Mind*, is next examined and found to be better than Husserl's in this respect. (In spite of chronology, Sartre treats this solution as if it were an improvement of Husserl's.) 'Here', he says, 'the appearance of the Other is indispensable, not to the constitution of the world and of my empirical ego, but to the very existence of my consciousness as self-consciousness. . . . It is only so far as each man is opposed to the Other that he is absolutely for himself. . . . Opposite the Other and confronting the Other, each one asserts his right of being individual.' Hegel says: 'Self-consciousness is real only in so far as it recognizes its echo and its reflection in another.' Out of this recognition of an echo and a reflection—a reflection without which, however, no original could exist—arises, according to Hegel, the notorious relation of Master to Slave—myself the Master, the Other the Slave. The opposition between myself and the Other is not theoretical only. It is an actual struggle between us. For I aim to have, as an integral cause of my self-consciousness, a being who is only this and nothing else—who exists, that is, for nothing except for me.

Here, then, is a crucial difference between Husserl's theory and Hegel's. Husserl was describing only how awareness of another person entered my consciousness. He was describing a permanent relation which held between my self and his. Hegel, on the other hand, was describing a dynamic situation, a struggle which goes on developing between myself and the Other. This actual struggle, which entails not merely knowing but acting, is essential, in his view, to the relation of one person to another.

At this point Sartre owes far more to Hegel than to Husserl; for it is an essential feature of the whole system of *Being and Nothingness* that it should be concerned not only, and not primarily, with knowing, but with doing and acting upon the world as well. So Sartre derives the failure of earlier philosophers to reach a satisfactory account of human relations from their insistence upon treating it as a purely epistemological question. On the contrary, he maintains, the point is to see how we necessarily act towards other human beings, and what our basic emotional attitude towards them must be; and if this is understood the problem of how we know that they exist alongside us will turn out to have been settled already. Here, to look ahead a bit, we can see how easily in the end Sartre would be able to adapt his philosophical outlook to Marxism. For Marxist philosophers insist that not *knowing* but *doing* is the point of philosophy; or rather that, human beings having the constitution they have, the way in which they get to know the world in which they live is by acting upon it. We shall come to this later. But already we can see in Sartre a rejection of pure epistemology. Striving, struggling, aiming, desiring, wishing, loving, and hating, all these are concepts which he finds it necessary to deploy in his description of our relation with others and with the world. Mere awareness is not enough.

(d) *Heidegger*

Finally Sartre considers Heidegger's account of human relations. Here there is a powerful move away from considering mere awareness, or perception, of others; for the basic notion which is used to explain human relations is not Being-for-others, but Being-*with*-others. I confess to finding Heidegger both unintelligible and unattractive, and Sartre's exposition of his theory is far from being, or even trying to be, clear. But, roughly speaking, the relation of *Being-with* is held to be not at all a matter of recognition of the existence of someone other than myself in the world, but entirely a matter of the manifest solidarity of the human contents of the world against the rest. 'It expresses . . . a sort of ontological solidarity for the exploitation of this world.' I am not to be thought of as face to face with another person whom I recognize as like myself. It is rather that I find myself dependent on other people in whatever I do.

In this condition of mutual interdependence, one does not necessarily realize the uniqueness of each individual person. Not to recognize uniqueness is to be, in Heidegger's terminology, in the 'unauthentic state'. In this state each is interchangeable with any other; and such a state is symbolized, or perhaps expressed, in my willingness, for instance, to wear ready-made clothes (which would do for anybody), to use public transport (designed for the convenience of anybody who wants it), to sit in public gardens, and so on. Each one comes to realize his own uniqueness when he contemplates his own death, which is the one thing necessarily unique for each of us. 'Authenticity and individuality have to be earned. I shall be my own authenticity only if, under the call of conscience, I launch out towards death . . . as towards my own most particular possibility. At this moment I reveal myself to myself in authenticity, and I raise others along with myself to the authentic.'

Luckily Sartre rejects this theory too, on the ground, mainly, that it is too abstract and general, too *a priori*, to help at all towards accounting for the precise, concrete relation between me and another concrete individual; and on the ground, also, that if I pretend that the concept of Being-with determines my relations with people in general this is an act of Bad Faith. Moreover, Heidegger's theory offers no kind of proof of the existence of others; and this is what Sartre is seeking to provide.

(3) The proof of the existence of others

From his consideration, and rejection, of all these theories, Sartre derives the conviction that whatever our relation with other people is we cannot lump people all together and try to define our consciousness of persons as a whole. We must seek to prove the existence for us of others, and our own existence for others, from a particular point of view—namely our own. We must always speak from a particular point of view: 'It is in principle impossible for us to adopt "the point of view of the whole".'

This is of the greatest importance in understanding what Sartre's proof of the existence of others amounts to, and indeed in understanding his philosophical method in general. A proof is, for him, a description so clear and vivid that, when I think of this description and fit it to my own case, I cannot fail to see its application. And in this case the description is going to be a description of how other people, individually, impinge upon my consciousness. The very best one can do in proving that I have a certain relation with the world, or with others, is to say what it is like being set down among them; how it seems, that is, from behind my eyes. If this is done well enough, it will be recognized by others as true for them too *mutatis mutandis*. But it is of no use whatever to attempt something which sets out to be a general statement. The particular description of my case must come first and may then be used as a description of another particular case, and then of another, and so on. But to attempt to describe the totality of human relations can never work.

This insistence on the particularity and concreteness of descriptions, from which ontological and metaphysical and general statements may be drawn, is what most clearly characterizes existentialist writing—and what, incidentally, makes it perfectly plausible for Sartre to use novels and plays as well as straight philosophical expositions to convey philosophical doctrines. We have here come, that is to say, upon the most important and characteristic demand which Sartre makes of philosophy, that it should be concrete, particular, and true to life. He believes that only after its descriptions have been recognized as true for *me* can they be used in the construction of a description of the world as a whole; that the statement of how things are in general can be attempted only through the recognition that this is how they inevitably are, when viewed from the point of view of a particular concrete person in the world.

It will be remembered that at the end of Part II of *Being and Nothingness* he said: 'If I want to describe in an exhaustive manner the relation of man to being . . .' This is what he does want, indeed what *Being and Nothingness* is an attempt to do. And we have, in his rejection of previous theories of human relations, come upon what he regards as an essential requirement of such an attempt—that it should be concrete. There is a special point in insisting on this demand, moreover, if we wish to understand the development of Sartre's philosophical thought. For in the end, as we shall see, it is just this particularity and concreteness which he is unable to preserve in the face of the powerful attraction of Marxism. And it may be that he was right to give it up. For, philosophically speaking, there *is* a difference between description, however vivid, and proof. The novelist or the film-director need not observe the distinction, but a philosopher must. It is the death of philosophy if it confuses the true with the convincing.

But for the time being, at any rate, the concrete and particular dictate the form of his theory of Being-for-others.

(4) How do we know that others exist?

In spite of his rejection of the epistemological approach to the problem, Sartre's own theory falls into two parts; the first an answer to the question how we know of the existence of others, the second to the question what we do when confronted with others.

First, then: How do we know? Briefly, Sartre's thesis is this: he argues that in our awareness of other people we do not first apprehend them as physical objects of a certain kind, and then argue, by analogy or in some other way, that they have consciousness, that they can feel and think; it is rather that our first apprehension of them strikes us as in some way *incomplete*. We have the feeling that, unlike other material objects which present themselves to us, here is one which can escape us, and indeed one which necessarily partially eludes us. This is not an inference from perception; neither is it a mysterious direct awareness of someone else's mind. It is, Sartre says, like ordinary perception with a hole in it. If I see a man in the park I see him not as *just* another material object, in a spatial relation to the other material objects which I see (though he *is* that as well). But I see him as an object which *organizes round itself* the other things which I see, not in a spatial relation, but in a relation of something like interest.

> Certainly the lawn remains six feet away from him, but is connected with him as well, *as a lawn*, in a relation that both transcends and contains distance. Instead of the two terms of distance being indifferent, interchangeable and reciprocal in relation to each other, the distance *unfolds* outwards from the man I can see *as far as* the lawn, like the synthetic emergence of a one-way relation. We are dealing with a relation *without parts*, given all in one, within which there unfolds a spatiality that is not *my* spatiality, for instead

74

of being a grouping of object towards me, it is an orientation which moves away from me.

So far, then, recognizing someone as another human being is recognizing that, unlike the other material objects in my field of vision, this one has the power to have his own, not my, point of view. But Sartre goes on: 'This relation without distance and without parts is in no way that original relation of the Other to me which I am seeking. In the first place it concerns only the man and the things in the world. Then it is still only an object of knowledge. I shall express it, for example, by saying that this man sees the lawn, or that in spite of the prohibiting sign, he is prepared to walk on the grass, and so on. Lastly it still retains a pure character of probability.' It is only probable, that is, that the object before me is a man, and that he sees the lawn and the *Keep Off the Grass* notice. 'Nevertheless', Sartre goes on, 'this new relation of the object-man to the object-lawn has a particular character; it is simultaneously given to me as a whole, since it is there in the world as an object which I can know, and at the same time it entirely escapes me. . . . To the extent that the relation *reaches towards him* it escapes me. I cannot put myself at the centre of it. So the first apprehension of another person is that something which is perceived by me as an object organizes round itself other things which I see. It escapes me "in as much as it unfolds about itself its own distances".'

This property which the Other has of escaping me is brought out still more clearly when we consider how I feel if the man I am watching is reading. In that case, Sartre says, 'it appears that the world has a kind of drain hole in the middle of its being, and that it is perpetually flowing off through this hole'. The man is describable as 'reading', just in the same way as a stone can be described as 'cold', or rain as 'fine'. 'Reading' is simply the name of the property that he has, for the time being. Yet 'the property "man reading" as the relation of the man to the book is a little particular crack in my universe. At the heart of this solid visible form, he makes himself a particular emptying.' The man escapes me, in that, however carefully I keep him in sight and try to have him as an object of attention, as I might have a stone or a tree as an object, I *cannot* read with his eyes, nor think what he thinks. The *massif* is nothing but an object for me; a man cannot be merely that.

But still this is not the whole truth about my relation with the Other. So far he still appears as an object for me, though of a unique and evasive kind. But the key to the peculiar relation between myself and the Other is that I am an object for him. He can look at me. I am not able to consider this fact exactly as I consider his looking at anything else, say the grass of the lawn, or his book. The difference is that being looked at by another actually affects and changes me myself. It makes me exist in a new way.

Sartre first considers the case of soldiers who are trying to escape the notice of the enemy. In this case they do not think of the look of the enemy as necessarily connected with any particular man whose eyes they can see looking at them. They regard bushes and trees, and all sorts of cover, as places from which the look may come. Perceiving the look of the other, then, is different from perceiving him as an object, or from perceiving his eyes. Indeed perceiving the look is incompatible with perceiving his eyes as objects. 'We cannot perceive the world and at the same time apprehend a look fixed upon us. It must be either one or the other. This is because to perceive is to look at; and to apprehend a look is not to apprehend a look-at-object in the world (unless the look is not directed upon us). It is to be conscious of *being looked at.*'

The next question, then, is what does it mean for me to be conscious of being looked at? This is answered by means of another example. I am, quite unself-consciously, and moved by overwhelming curiosity or jealousy, looking into a room through the keyhole. I am 'at the level of non-reflective self-consciousness'—that is, I am aware of the keyhole, and of my interest, but I am not aware of myself as a separate

object. I could not criticize my action at this stage. 'I am
my acts, and hence they carry in themselves their whole
justification.' I am not thinking of myself as eavesdropping,
I am just eavesdropping. 'But all of a sudden I hear foot-
steps in the hall. Someone is looking at me. What does this
mean? It means that I am suddenly affected in my being,
and that essential modifications appear in my structure . . .
modifications which I can apprehend and fix conceptually
by means of the reflective *cogito*.' I suddenly become for
myself exactly and only what I appear to the Other. But I
do not reject how-I-appear-to-the-Other as a strange image,
having no connexion with myself. On the contrary, as we
have seen earlier, I recognize myself in the image which the
Other has of me, in shame. 'It is shame or pride which
reveals to me the Other's look and myself at the end of that
look. It is the shame or pride which makes me *live*, not
merely know, the situation of being looked at. Now shame,
as we noted at the beginning of the chapter, is shame of
self. It is the recognition of the fact that I am indeed the
object which the Other is looking at and judging. I can be
ashamed only as my freedom escapes me in order to become
a *given* object. Beyond any knowledge that I can have, I
am this self which another knows. And this self which I
am . . . this I am in a world which the Other has made
alien from me.'

For the look of the Other embraces all the things about
me, the walls, the door, the keyhole, and makes them *his*
instead of mine, as they were before, when I was alone. All
the things which were merely instruments or obstacles *for
me*, now turn towards the Other an aspect which I cannot,
and necessarily cannot, apprehend. Things which were
nothing but my possibilities become alienated from me;
and at the same time I become thing-like myself, since in the
eyes of the Other I am bending over the keyhole just as a
tree is bending over the river, or an ink-well is on the table.
For myself, I was nothing but my plans and purposes and
interests; that is to say, my free actions. For the Other I
am an object in his world. 'Thus in the shock which seizes

me when I apprehend the Other's look this happens, that suddenly I experience a subtle alienation of all my possibilities, which are now associated with objects of the world, far from me, in the midst of the world.'

(5) Consequences of being looked at

There are, then, two main consequences of my apprehending the look of the Other. First of all, as an object of the Other's look, I am a thing, not wholly determined, doubtless, but to be judged in terms of probability like many other objects in the world, for instance like the weather. I may feel that I can myself determine what I will do next, that I can state my intentions and carry them out. The Other will judge me inductively, as he judges the behaviour of animals, or the probable development of plants. He may or may not be moved by my avowed intentions. Since I am an object for him, he has his own methods of assessing my probable behaviour. I am thing-like in his eyes, and things cannot make promises. 'Later, when we gradually learn what the Other thinks of us, this is the thing which will be able at once to fascinate us and fill us with horror. "I swear to you I will do it." "Maybe so, you tell me so. I want to believe you. It is indeed possible that you will do it." ' This dreadful little dialogue brings out the difference between my view of my possibilities and his. For him I have no possibilities of my own making. I am a thing which may or may not behave in the way I say I will. My promises are only a special kind of predictions, and may be falsified as well as any others. His guess is as good as mine.

This difference between the attitudes of ourselves to ourselves and of other people to ourselves seems to me to have enormous importance not only in determining how we describe our behaviour, but also in affecting how we actually behave. It also brings clearly to light a whole number of decisions which we familiarly have to make concerning our treatment of others. When do we stop pretending to take their promises seriously? How soon do we make it clear to them that we regard them as entirely mistaken about what they will do, no matter what their present intentions are? The decisions of this kind which we take do in fact very often affect, for good or ill, the degree to which people *can* choose to behave in one way rather than another.

The second consequence is that, once I am aware of the Other, I realize that I am not wholly master of the situation. There is at once something in it which, in principle, eludes me, namely the Other's thoughts. Things may *be done* to me which I do not understand; there can be a kind of Kafka-like quality in real life, but only when I think of myself as under the gaze of the Other.

There are certain further corollaries of this failure to be able totally to control my situation. I am, in the eyes of the Other, an object not merely of perception but also of appraisal. He is free to judge me, and I am in perpetual danger of being labelled and type-cast in some role not of my choosing. The fact that this labelling is reciprocal, and that I can cast the Other in some role which he might not have chosen, makes no difference; paying him in his own coin does not in the slightest reduce the danger for me. I may, of course wish to avail myself of his labels, and shuffle off my responsibility for what I am, by simply being what he says I am. This, as we have seen, is Bad Faith. Genet, the thief, became a thief because he was called one. But if I do not wish to sink into Bad Faith, I see the judgment of the Other as his means of enslaving me.

In this disagreeable situation I make use of such defence as I can, and the only defence available to me is to try to destroy this unknown freedom of the Other, by making a thing of him. The Other is, as we have seen, revealed to me in the first place not just as an object of perception, but as that by whom I am regarded—as the source of 'the look'. If I can come to think of the Other as a mere object of perception then to a certain extent my danger is mitigated, or at least made bearable. But to treat him as an object, though it may be my sole defence, cannot be entirely successful. For not only do I first learn of the Other through his look at me, but in doing so I learn at the same time that he is free—free, for instance, to make what appraisal he likes of me.

Now there is no obstacle more final to my projects and plans than the freedom of someone else. To be impeded by physical objects is far less terrible than to be impeded by the free will of somebody else. And as the Other is in fact free, treating him as though he were an object and not a free person cannot be more than a pretence. 'To remain at home because it is raining and to remain at home because one has been forbidden to go out are by no means the same thing. . . . It is not mere caprice which causes us often to do very naturally and without annoyance what would irritate us if another commanded it. This is because the order and the prohibition cause us to experience the Other's freedom and our own slavery. Thus in "the look" the death of my possibilities causes me to experience the Other's freedom.'

The manner in which we come to be aware of the Other, concretely, as a freedom inhibiting our own, explains why we all of us have a native and irresistible tendency to reject the arguments of solipsism as nonsense. 'This resistance is indeed based on the fact that the Other is given to me as a concrete evident presence which I can in no way derive from myself and which can in no way be placed in doubt. . . .' My awareness of the Other is not just knowledge, but in itself a way of striving against something, as one might say that awareness of danger of other sorts is not mere knowledge, but already and immediately a struggle to escape. 'The fact of the Other is incontestable and touches me to the heart. I realize him through uneasiness; through him I am perpetually in danger in a world which is this world, and which nevertheless I only glimpse. The Other does not appear to me as a being who is constituted first, so as to encounter me later; he appears as a being who arises in an original relation of being with me, and whose indubitability and factual necessity are those of my own consciousness.'

With a few more elaborations this is the answer which Sartre gives to the question 'How do we know the existence of other minds?' And the foundation is thereby laid for the answer to the further question of our fundamental relation with other people—the question, that is, of how we necessarily behave towards them. For no one who has read so far, and who has discovered the existence of the Other as a perpetual obstacle to my freedom, and as constituting my danger, will be surprised to learn that our relations with one another in general are characterized by an extreme hostility, and by perpetual struggle.

(6) How do we treat other people?

The problem of our relations to each other is posed in the form 'What is my Body?' and 'What is the Body of the Other?' These questions occupy the second chapter of Part III of *Being and Nothingness*.

My body, Sartre says, is my contact with the world. It constitutes my contingency. It is not entirely clear, as we shall see later, what this means. But Sartre seems to be saying that though it is entirely *necessary* for a consciousness which is a consciousness of the world to have some body, it is contingent for each of us what body we have, where we are born, and, in general, how we are located among other physical objects. When Sartre says that we need a body in order to perceive the world he is careful to insist that he does not mean that we use our bodies as *instruments* of perception. For this would presuppose the priority of mind over body. In fact it is not that the world is revealed to us through the body. Rather, we are orginally and necessarily in a certain relation with the world, which reveals our body to us. 'The body is not a screen between ourselves and things; it manifests only the individuality and the contingency of our original relation to instrumental things.' Using my body, for example using my eyes to see with, is, Sartre says, going beyond them towards what I see. This is not entirely clear: but it seems to refer to the fact that, when I use my eyes, I am not conscious of my eyes but only of what falls within my field of vision; and whatever falls within my field of vision is seen by me as part of *my* plans and projects and of *my* route through the world. In the same way, if I use my hands to untie a knot, I am not particularly conscious of my hands; I concentrate on the knot, and upon this only as an obstacle to something else, namely opening the parcel.

Sartre gives the perhaps tendentious example of reading (which, as we have seen, he has used before to illustrate a similar point) to show how mere perception is not something which rests upon the object, or upon the organ, but always goes beyond either, to the construction of some larger whole. But even if this is thought to be rather a special case it is clear enough that Sartre wishes to place our awareness of our own body in a special category of knowledge; and from this he draws conclusions about our awareness of, and treatment of, others.

Our eyes and hands and ears—our body in general—constitute for us our own particular point of view. This is why we cannot adopt the point of view of the whole; each of us is saddled with the insistent presence of his own body. 'In each project of the For-itself, in each perception, the body is there, it is the immediate past in so far as it still touches on the present which flees it. This means that it is at once a point of view, and a point of departure . . . a point of view, a point of departure which I am, and which at the same time I go beyond, towards what I have to be.' This constant awareness of our own body has, as we shall see, its special, and, for Sartre, disagreeable flavour, which determines how we see the world in general. We shall have something to say about this in the next chapter. For the moment we are concerned with the fact that other people have bodies too.

Now just as my own body is revealed to me partly by my going beyond it in action (as well as in perception), so other people's bodies cannot be distinguished by me from their actions. Their bodies are the 'objective contingency' of their actions. I cannot see first a hand which might take hold of a glass, and then notice that there is in fact a glass in this hand. My perception of the glass and the hand are indissolubly one; and this is not just the mere accident that I catch sight of them both together. It is that I *interpret* the hand as that which is meant for picking things up; and the fact that here before me is a flesh-and-blood hand is precisely what puts me in the situation I am in, sitting opposite my friend Pierre in the café.

Once again, Sartre shows himself almost obsessively concerned with the particular and the concrete. If we can understand in exactly what way we are aware of the friend who now sits opposite us, and how we see him, then we shall have understood the solution to the problem of our relation with other people. For my perception of the body of another person is unique, and entirely distinct from my perception of any other material thing whatever, in that each movement that he makes is seen as *meaning something*, and as 'goal-directed'. We see the body of another person as what he is, because we see what he plans and intends. Even our knowledge of the character of another person is arrived at through the apprehension of his body; for instance, I am acquainted with a man's irascibility through my knowledge of his appearance, and for me his irascibility is necessarily grounded on how he looks and moves.

So far, then, we have been shown in what way I exist as a body for myself, in what way the Other exists as a body for me, and in what way I exist as a body for the Other. These three aspects of the existence of body lead to the final discussion of the concrete relations between one person and another which occupies Chapter 3 of this third part.

The basic facts are these. The Other possesses me by looking at me, for in this way he creates me as a person. At the same time I seek to possess him. 'While I attempt to free myself from the hold of the Other, the Other is trying to free himself from mine; while I seek to enslave the Other, the Other seeks to enslave me. We are by no means dealing with unilateral relations with an object-in-itself, but with reciprocal and moving relations. . . . Descriptions of concrete behaviour must therefore be seen within the perspective of *conflict*. Conflict is the original meaning of Being-for-others.'

Of course, it is a conflict in which neither of us can ever succeed. For what I want to get hold of is the Other's freedom. It is of no use to me to possess him if he is not still a free human being when he is mine. If I killed him I should in a way possess him, but since he would no longer be free this would not satisfy me. But if he is free then he necessarily escapes me. I cannot control what he thinks or what he plans to do. A free and conscious being cannot be possessed. This is most clearly illustrated in the particular relation of love. It is in this relation that the whole of Being-for-others is epitomized, and I shall quote the long passage in which this is described.

'It is in this sense that love is a conflict: We have observed that the Other's freedom is the foundation of my being. But precisely because I exist by means of the Other's freedom I have no security; I am in danger in this freedom. It moulds my being and makes me be, it confers values upon it and removes it from me; and my being receives from it a perpetual passive escape from self. Irresponsible and beyond reach, this protean freedom in which I have engaged myself can in turn engage me in a thousand different ways of being. My project of recovering my being can be realized only if I get hold of this freedom, and reduce it to being a freedom subject to my freedom. . . . Why does the lover want to be *loved*? If love were in fact a pure desire for physical possession it could in many cases be satisfied. Proust's hero, for instance, who installs his mistress in his house, who can see her and possess her at any hour of the day, ought to be free from worry. Yet we know that he is, on the contrary, continually gnawed by anxiety. Through her consciousness, Albertine escapes Marcel, even when he is at her side, and that is why he knows relief only when he gazes on her while she sleeps. It is certain, then, that the lover wishes to capture a consciousness. But why does he wish it? and how? The notion of "ownership" by which love is so often explained is not actually primary. Why should I want to appropriate the Other, if it were not precisely that the Other makes me be? But this implies precisely a certain mode of appropriation: it is the Other's freedom, as such, that we want to get hold of. Not because of a desire for power. The tyrant scorns love, he is content with fear. If he seeks to win the love of his subjects it is for political reasons; and if he finds a more economical way to enslave them he adopts it immediately. On the other hand the man who wants to be loved does not desire the enslavement of the beloved. He is not bent on becoming the object of a devotion which flows forth mechanically. He does not want to possess an automaton, and if we want to humiliate him we need only try to persuade him that the beloved's passion is a result of psychological determinism. The lover will then feel that both his love and his being are cheapened. If Tristan and Isolde fall madly in love because of a love-potion, they are less interesting. The total enslavement of the beloved kills the love of the lover. If the beloved is transformed into an automaton the lover finds himself alone. Thus the lover does not desire to possess the beloved as one possesses a thing; he demands a special type of appropriation. He wants to possess freedom as freedom. On the other hand, the lover cannot be satisfied with the superior form of freedom which is a free and voluntary engagement. Who would be content with a love given as pure loyalty to a sworn oath? Who would be satisfied with the words "I love you because I have freely engaged myself to love you and because I do not wish to go back on my word"? Thus the lover demands a pledge, but is irritated by the pledge. He wants to be loved by freedom, but demands that this freedom should no longer be free. . . . He is, and consents to be, an object. But . . . he wants to be the object in which the Other's freedom consents to lose itself . . . he does not want to act on the Other's freedom, but to exist, *a priori*, as the objective limit to this freedom. . . .' This struggle upon which the lovers embark, each to possess the freedom of the Other, and yet to be freely loved, is, of course, hopeless, for it is based on the contradictory assumption that a person can be both free and a slave.

And, being hopeless, it may lead only to three different patterns of behaviour, all directed in vain towards the same hopeless end. In the first place it may lead to masochism. This is defined by Sartre as the state in which I consent to be nothing but an object for the beloved; but I am led thereby not only to guilt, but to frustration, since in my own eyes I cannot be nothing but an object; I still always have free choices of my own to make. It is impossible for me to lose myself entirely in Being-for-the-Other. I have Being-for-myself as well. Secondly, I may adopt the attitude of indifference. I may choose simply to observe the behaviour of the Other. Or, thirdly, I may attempt the immediate appropriation of the Other by violence, and this is sadism. But none of these devices can satisfy me in the end.

(7) Summary

At the end of Part III Sartre sums up his conclusions so far. There is, to start with, the basic distinction between things-in-themselves and the For-itself, or conscious being. The In-itself has no within which is opposed to a without. Conscious being, on the other hand, considered in isolation, is nothing except a within, an emptiness to be filled up. But the encounter of one conscious being with another gives the For-itself an outside. Other people *see* us and fix us with their look and make objects in the world out of us all. We become things among other things. 'This petrifaction of the In-itself by the Other's look is the profound meaning', he says, 'of the myth of Medusa.' But there is a further characteristic of the For-itself which has so far been only incidentally considered, and that is its possibility of acting upon things-in-themselves. How is such action possible? Sartre concludes that by the end of the third part of *Being and Nothingness* he has accumulated all the material for answering this question. But for our purposes we must go back a bit. For before we discuss his view of the nature of free action, perhaps the most important subject in the book, it is necessary to look a little more at what he thinks is the general nature of the world of things, on the 'flesh' of which human beings make their effect in action. It is therefore to the general characteristics of the world of things that we turn in the next chapter.

4

Being-in-the-world

(1) The paradox of particularity

When we begin to consider Sartre's account of the character-istics of the world in which consciousness has its 'upsurge' we are immediately confronted by a paradox, the nature of which I hinted at briefly in Part 3. Sartre is concerned to pin down the particular. Each one of us, but also each object in the world around us, has his own 'facticity', that is to say his own unique position; and, as far as human beings are concerned, each necessarily has his own point of view. Part of the essential task of philosophy is to describe what it is like to experience something; and the philosopher must learn to put on one side all presuppositions and habitual modes of classification of experience, so that he can say truly what they are like. This is what Sartre learned from the phenomenologists' *epoche*, by which the world is put into brackets. Giving this kind of description entails concentrating on *one* thing, *one* experience, or *one* object at a time; and the secret of successful description is not to take one's attention from the particular thing by comparing it with other things, nor light-heartedly to hope to name it and pass on to something else. Simone de Beauvoir records how Sartre when quite a young man met someone at a café, who, looking at a bottle on the table between them, said that what he wanted was a philosophy of things, and how Sartre felt an immediate sympathy with this desire. To reach the truth we must keep our eyes on some one concrete object.

We know, then, that this is what Sartre hoped to do.

Yet the paradox is this: besides wanting to come at the particular in quite a new way, he thought that philosophy is metaphysical—that is, that it should provide a total and universal account of the nature of the world, such that whatever phenomenon one picks on, this is accounted for by assigning it its right place in the whole. Though Sartre knows that we each perceive the world, irrevocably, through our own eyes, yet he wishes to say that we *must* perceive it as we do in one way rather than another.

Now this paradox is familiar to philosophers. Kant was concerned with this very adjustment of the subjective to the objective and necessary in our statements about the world and our categorizing of it. But subjectivity for Kant was less extreme than for Sartre; and objectivity was more systematic. Sartre tries to tell us what the world is like in general, without providing a system, but merely by extending his description of the particular vaguely and indefinitely outwards. We are inevitably left with the question why things should be as he says, and with the feeling that as a matter of fact they are not, or only accidentally. This is almost to say that, so far as this aspect of his philosophy goes, Sartre is not really, or only accidentally, a philosopher. For philosophy must be general, whereas what Sartre gives us is a description of the particular which has as its aim to make us *feel* the particularity of things; and this we may reasonably believe to be the province of, say, poetry or the cinema rather than of philosophy. When he tries to construct the general account out of the material of the particular he fails. All we have is exaggeration, rather than true generality. Kant's categories might make some serious claim to be a list of the elements of the structure of our world; at least he tries to *deduce* them. Sartre's general account of the world, on the other hand, has no *rationale*. It is as if someone who, in a novel, successfully made us feel what it was like to be, for instance, jealous, or depressed, then said, 'and we are all of us in this state all the time'. But, of course, though we can understand the state, we *know* that we are not in it all the time. And the success even of the particular description is rendered suspect if, after all, we are told that it is not really particular but entirely general.

(2) 'La Nausée'

It is no accident that we find the most powerful account of the nature and particularity of things in one of Sartre's novels; and into the long passage which I shall quote are woven all the main elements out of which Sartre's general description of the world is to be constructed.

The passage comes towards the end of *La Nausée*, and is part of a long and dramatic entry in Roquentin's diary. It is a description of the condition of nausea, which Roquentin had come to be familiar with, to describe which, indeed, was the original purpose of his diary.

> The Nausea hasn't left me and I think it will be some time before it does: but I don't suffer from it any more, it is no longer an illness or a passing fit: it is I.
>
> For instance, I was in the public park just now. The horse-chestnut tree root went down into the ground just under my bench. I could no longer remember that it was a root. The words had vanished and with them the meaning of things, their uses, the insignificant points of reference that men have traced on their surfaces. I was sitting down, stooping a little, with my head bowed, alone in face of this black, knotted, entirely crude mass which frightened me. And then I had a sudden illumination.
>
> It took my breath away. I had never, until these last few days, suspected what 'to exist' meant. I had been like other people, like those who go walking by the sea in their new spring outfits. I used to say, like them, 'the sea *is* green, that white speck up there *is* a seagull': but I never felt that these things existed, that the sea-gull was an 'existing-seagull': normally, existence is hidden. It is there, all round us, in us, it is us, we can't say two words without mentioning it, and yet you can't

touch it. I must believe that, when I believed I was thinking about it. I wasn't thinking about anything, that my head was empty, or that there was just one word in it, the word 'to be'. Or else, I was thinking— how shall I put it? I was thinking about *belonging*. I was saying to myself that the sea belonged to the class of green objects, or that green was one of the qualities of the sea. Even when I looked at these things I was miles from thinking that they existed: they seemed to me like stage scenery. I took them in my hands, they served as tools, and I could gauge their resistance. But all that was happening on the surface. If anyone had asked me what existence was, I should have replied, in all good faith, that it wasn't anything, just an empty form which was added to external things without in any way changing their nature. But suddenly there it was, as clear as day: existence was suddenly revealed. It had lost its inoffensive look of an abstract category: it was the very stuff of things. This root had been moulded in existence. Or rather, the root, the park railings, the bench, the sparse grass on the lawn, all these things had disappeared: the diversity, the individuality of things was a mere illusion, a veneer. The veneer had splintered, leaving monstrous, flabby, disorganized masses—naked, terrifyingly, obscenely naked.

I kept myself from making the slightest movement, but I had no need to move to be able to see, behind the trees, the blue pillars and the candelabrum of the bandstand, and the Velleda in the middle of a clump of laurels. All these objects—how can I put it? They disturbed me. I should have liked them to exist less hard, in a drier, more abstract way, with more reserve. The horse-chestnut tree pressed up against my eyes. Its bottom half was covered with a green mildew: the bark, black and bloated, was like boiled leather. The soft splashing of the fountain crept into my ears and made itself a nest there, filling them with whispering noises: my nostrils overflowed with a green, putrid smell. Everything was abandoning itself softly, tenderly to existence, like those worn-out women who give themselves up to unrestrained laughter, and say 'It's nice to have a good laugh' in a sodden voice: they sprawled out in front of each other, giving away the abject secrets of their existence. I saw that there was no middle term between non-existence and this swooning abundance. If anything existed, it had to exist to this point, to the point of rottenness, bloatedness, obscenity. In another world, arches and tunes keep their pure and rigid lines. But existence is a deflection. Trees, midnight blue pillars, the happy gurgling of a fountain, living scents, little vapours of warmth floating in the cold air, a red-haired man digesting on a bench: all this somnolence, all these digestive processes taken together had a vaguely comical side. No, not comical, rather it was an indeterminate, almost entirely elusive analogy with certain situations in farce. We were a heap of existing things, hindered and by ourselves, we had not the slightest reason for being here, not one of us, each existing thing, confused and vaguely troubled, felt superfluous in relation to the others. Superfluous: it was the only connexion I could establish between the trees, the railings, the gravel. I tried vainly to count the horse-chestnut trees, to *place* them in relation to the Velleda, to compare them in height with the plane-trees. Every one of them eluded the web of connexion in which I tried to imprison it, isolated itself and overflowed. I felt how arbitrary were these connexions (which I insisted on maintaining in order to put off the collapse of the human world, measures, quantities and directions): they no longer established a hold on things. Superfluous, that horse-chestnut tree opposite me and a little to the left. The Velleda, superfluous.

And as for me—flabby, languid, obscene, digesting, aimlessly juggling with dreary thoughts—I too am

superfluous. Fortunately I didn't feel it. I knew it
more, but I was uncomfortable because I was afraid of
feeling it. (Even now I am afraid—I am afraid it might
catch me by the back of my head and lift me up like a
ground-swell.) I thought vaguely of doing away with
myself. So that at least one of these superfluous lives
would be annihilated. But even my death would have
been superfluous. Superfluous, my corpse, my blood on
the gravel, amongst these plants, in the heart of this
radiant garden. And my decomposed flesh would have
been superfluous in the earth that received it, and
finally my bones, cleaned, stripped bare, clean and
spotless as teeth would still have been superfluous: I
was superfluous to eternity.

The word 'Absurdity' comes to my pen at present:
just now, in the park I couldn't find it, but then I
wasn't looking for it. I didn't need it: I thought without words, on to things, with things. 'Absurdity' wasn't
an idea in my head or the sound of a voice, but that
long dead snake at my feet, that snake of wood. Snake
or claw or root or vulture's talon, it makes no difference.
And without formulating anything clearly I realized
that I had discovered the key to Existence, the key to
my fits of Nausea and the key to my own life. Indeed,
anything I have managed to apprehend since leads
back to the same basic absurdity. 'Absurdity': another
word: I fight against words: down there in the park I
touched the thing. But I should like here and now to
fix the absolute nature of this absurdity. An act or an
event in the little brightly coloured world of men is
never more than relatively absurd: in relation to the
accompanying circumstances. The ravings of a madman,
for example, are absurd in relation to his situation,
but not in relation to his delirium. But I, just now,
have experienced the absolute: the absolute or absurd.
Take that root—there was nothing in relation to which
it would not have been absurd. Oh! how can I put that
into words? Absurd: in relation to the gravel, the

tufts of yellow grass, the dried mud, the tree, the sky, the green benches. Absurd, irreducible: nothing, not even some secret deep-down madness in nature could explain it. Clearly I didn't know everything: I hadn't seen the seed develop or the tree grow: but both ignorance and knowledge were irrelevant in the face of that great gnarled paw.

The world of explanations and reasons is not the world of existence. A circle isn't absurd—it can be perfectly satisfactorily explained as the rotations of a segment of a straight line round one of its extremities. But then a circle doesn't exist. On the other hand the root existed just in so far as I couldn't explain it. Knotted, inert, nameless, it fascinated me, filled my eyes, drew me continually back to its own existence. In vain I repeated 'that is a root'—it didn't catch on any more. I saw clearly that you couldn't go from its function as a root, as a suction-pump to *that*, that hard, dense seal-like skin, that oily, callous, stubborn appearance. Its function didn't explain anything: it allowed you to come to a general understanding of what a root is, but not in the least what that particular one was. That root, with its colour, shape, and petrified motion was beneath all explanation. Each of its qualities over-flowed a little, trickled out of it, half solidified, almost became a thing: each of them was to excess in the root, and the whole stump now gave one the impression of moving slightly out of itself, rejecting itself and losing its identity in a strange superabundance. I scraped my heel against the black claw: I wanted to peel off some of the bark. Not for any reason, but out of defiance, to make the ridiculous pinkness of a scratch appear on its tanned hide: to play with the absurdity of the world. But when I took my foot away I saw that the bark was still black.

Black? I felt the word deflate, empty itself of meaning with extraordinary speed. Black? The root was not black, there was no black on that piece of wood—

there was—something else: blackness, like the circle, didn't exist. I looked at the root: was it *blacker than black* or *nearly* black? But I soon stopped wondering, because I had the impression of being on familiar ground. Yes. I had examined unnameable objects with the same anxiety before. I had attempted vainly to think something *on to them* before: I had felt their cold inert qualities slip through my fingers before. Adolphe's braces, the other evening, at the 'Railwaymen's Arms'. They *were not* purple. I saw again the two indefinable spots of colour on his shirt. And the pebble, the famous pebble, the beginning of the whole story. It wasn't—I couldn't quite remember what it refused to be. But I hadn't forgotten its passive resistance. And the Self-Taught man's hand. I had taken it and shaken it one day in the library and then I had felt that it wasn't altogether a hand. I thought of it as a great white grub, but it wasn't entirely that either. And the dubious transparency of beer at the Café Mably. Dubious, that's what they were, sounds, smells, tastes. When things passed rapidly under your nose like hares you have started, without your paying very much attention to them you could believe them to be quite simple and reassuring, you could believe that there was real blue, real red, a real smell of almonds and violets in the world. But as soon as you hung on to them for a moment the feeling of comfort and security gave way to profound uneasiness: colours, tastes, smells were never real, never just themselves and nothing but themselves. The simplest and most undecomposable quality had a superfluous element in it in relation to itself, at its heart. The black at my foot didn't look like black, but rather a muddled effort to imagine black by someone who had never seen black and who had imagined an equivocal entity over and above colours. It was *like* a colour, but also like a bruise or a secretion, an oozing—and like something else, a smell for example, it merged into the smell of

damp earth, of warm, damp wood, into the taste of
chewed sugary fibre. I didn't simply *see* the black.
Sight is an abstract invention, a neatened-up, simplified
idea, one of man's inventions. This blackness, an
amorphous flabby presence, overflowed the bounds of
sight, taste, and smell. But its richness turned into
confusion and eventually became nothing, through
being too much.

That was an extraordinary moment. I stood there,
motionless and transfixed, plunged into a horrible
ecstasy. But in the very midst of this ecstasy something
new had just emerged. I understood Nausea, I possessed
it. To tell the truth I didn't formulate my discoveries.
But I think that now it would be easy to put them into
words. The essential thing is contingency. I mean that
by definition existence is not necessity. To exist is
simply *to be there*: existing things appear, let themselves
be *encountered*, but one can never *deduce* them. I
think there are people who have understood this.
Only they tried to overcome contingency by inventing
a necessary being, a self-caused cause. Now no necessary being can explain existence: contingency isn't an
illusion or a mere appearance that can be dissipated:
it is the absolute, and thus the perfect inconsequent:
everything is inconsequential, the park, the town, and
myself: when you realize that, it turns your stomach
and everything begins to seem like the other evening
at the 'Railwayman's Arms'. That is Nausea: that is
what those bastards—at the 'Green Hill' and others—
try to hide from themselves with their notions of rights.
But what a pathetic lie—no one has the right: they
are utterly inconsequential like other men, but they
cannot succeed in feeling superfluous. And inside
themselves, secretly, they *are superfluous* to excess,
that is, amorphous, vague, and wretched.

I have quoted from this early novel at great length, for
there are here all the elements of the description of the

world which Sartre was to give in *Being and Nothingness*; and the way in which the description is first given, here, is of great importance. For it arose, as we have seen, from the contemplation of one particular thing, a tree root, and grew finally until it was general. The description applied not to abstract, definable entities, but to concrete, indefinable things. Existence itself, the world, was like this, and could be seen to be so.

But, still, Roquentin, it may be argued, was an individual, and a fictitious one at that. Just because he thought he had discovered the nature of the world are we to take this over? Roquentin's Nausea was his own particular disease. We do not have to suppose that everybody shares it, nor need we even think that Sartre believes this. And this is true. One cannot derive a metaphysical description from the words of the character in a novel, by themselves. But these words do in fact make more explicit and immediate what is contained, though with less detail, elsewhere, and when we turn to *Being and Nothingness* we realize that Roquentin was, in this passage at least, supposed to be speaking for all of us. The three feelings which we must all of us experience when we reflect upon the world are nausea, a sense of the absurd, or of our own superfluity, and anguish. We shall consider these feelings in turn.

(3) Nausea

First, then, Nausea. Roquentin came to understand that nausea was part of himself, indeed that it *was* himself, in relation to other things and other people. Nausea is our most primitive and original feeling about the world, for we cannot experience anything without experiencing this. We may sometimes avoid awareness of nausea by submerging it in particular desires and projects, and in particular feelings and sensations. But if it is not submerged we can be aware of it all the time. This is because nausea is our awareness of ourselves, or, rather, of our own bodies, without which we cannot be aware of anything else at all.

D

Nausea is the physical counterpart of the 'cogito' of Descartes. If I am aware of the world I must also, in a minimal sense, be aware of the body, by means of which I have my contact with the world in perception. And this minimal awareness is nausea.

Consciousness without some awareness of the body to which it is contingently attached, to which it belongs, would not be capable of being consciousness of the world. For I must be aware of the world as *physical* through that part of me which is physical. My body is my contact with the world, and so awareness of the world must always be mediated through some kind of awareness of my body. Sartre writes: 'In particular we must note than when no pain, no specific satisfaction or dissatisfaction is "existed" (i.e. experienced or "lived through") by consciousness, the For-itself does not thereby cease to project itself beyond a contingency which is pure and so to speak unqualified. Consciousness does not cease to "have" a body. . . . This perpetual apprehension, on the part of my For-itself, of an *insipid* taste which I cannot place, which accompanies me even in my efforts to get away from it, and which is *my* taste . . . this is what we have described elsewhere under the name of nausea. A dull and inescapable nausea perpetually reveals my body to my consciousness. Sometimes we look for the pleasant or for physical pain to free ourselves from this nausea; but as soon as the pain or the pleasure are experienced by consciousness they in turn manifest its facticity and its contingency; and it is against the background of this nausea that they are revealed.'

It is very important to notice that Sartre does not mean nausea to be taken as a metaphorical description of our attitude to the world, nor as an exaggeration. He intends us to understand that we actually and literally feel this nausea, necessarily, in our apprehension of the world, even though we may sometimes forget it. And the reason for this is in the nature of the world itself. Nausea arises because the world is as it is. Perhaps we are meant to suppose that, in some other imaginable world, we might have had some different reaction. But though we can imagine this in theory, in practice we cannot even think it, since the characteristic which makes the world nauseous to us is fundamental to the only world we have ever known.

It is necessary here to remind ourselves of what Sartre believes the emotions to be. All emotions and all feelings are modes of apprehension of the world; they are essentially ways of being aware of things. Therefore if one says that one feels disgust this feeling is a manner of apprehending a disgusting object. To say 'I feel disgust' needs to be completed by my saying what it is that disgusts me. When this is said I shall have described both my feeling, and its object, at one and the same time. All the emotions share this feature. For example, if I say 'I am afraid', I can complete this by saying what it is that I fear, and when I do this I am saying that this object *is threatening*—that I apprehend its threatening nature as one of its properties. Now it is possible to list the fundamental properties which objects may have—physical objects, that is. And if we took the properties of objects more seriously we should at the same time come to see why we are affected by them as we are. One of the fundamental categories of which we must make use in our description of things in the world is the 'visqueux'; and it is apprehending the viscosity of things which is identical with apprehending them as nauseating. Sartre speaks here, incidentally, of a psycho-analysis of things, and he suggests that if we attended to things in detail we should see why, for instance, a particular person may find eggs disgusting or may like the texture or appearance of peppers. He is here, obviously, borrowing from Freud. Though his explanations are not like Freud's, the concept of such an enterprise is purely Freudian.

(4) The viscous

It is difficult to find a single English word which is exactly right as a translation of 'visqueux'. 'Slimy' and 'sticky' have both been suggested. I shall use 'viscous' and hope to establish the exact meaning of this by means of examples. Probably the most obviously 'viscous' thing, in Sartre's sense, is treacle. Treacle has the characteristic, essential to the viscous, of being semi-liquid. It is not solid but it offers a resistance greater than water. It is sticky and soft. It has no shape of its own, but it does not flow away entirely. This kind of substance, Sartre claims, exerts a peculiar fascination on us, as well as filling us with disgust. Moreover we do not have to be taught to regard it in this way; our attitude is absolutely natural and instinctive. As soon as we become aware of objects in the world at all we are aware of the fascination and horror of the viscous. As children, our world is filled with mud, slime, treacle, honey, and other such dreadful things. The key to our emotional awareness of viscosity (and, as we have seen, our emotions cannot be separated from our perceptions) is its natural *ambiguity*. Lying as it does halfway between the liquid and the solid, it deceives us, whichever way we choose to regard it. We think that we can touch it, and pick it up, like a solid, but it eludes us; it has no boundaries. On the other hand, if we try to pour it away like water it refuses to go. If I touch it, Sartre says, 'at the very moment when I believe that I possess it, by a curious reversal, it possesses me'. For it sticks to my hands, and I cannot get rid of it.

In the part of *Being and Nothingness* entitled 'Quality as a revelation of Being' (Part IV, Chapter 2, Section 3) Sartre devotes many pages to a description of the viscosity of things, and to an explanation of how it is that we necessarily use the viscous as a symbol of the nature of the world in general. For we do so use it, though we are not taught to. The viscous is an important category for us to employ in our descriptions of the world just because it does, in itself, stand for our relation with things-in-themselves. We desire to possess them, but they elude us. We want to control them, but we find that they frequently control us. We want to tidy them up, docket them, label them, give them hard edges so that we can pin them down, once and for all, with a word or a classification, but we find that they escape our language. Their edges are blurred, they flow away from what we want to say about them. We come to fear the recalcitrance of the world of things, and we have a terror of being submerged in it so completely that all our plans and projects would go for nothing. Here again, the full impact of the point which Sartre is making cannot be felt without quotation. I shall quote at length, but, even so, all these words are only a tiny fraction of the great flood of words he lets flow to convey his horror and disgust at the world.

He says that the viscous is a natural symbol, one which we use whether we want to or not, and then he asks:

What mode of being is symbolized by the viscous? I see first that it is the homogeneity and the imitation of liquidity. A viscous substance like pitch is an aberrant fluid. At first, with the appearance of a fluid it manifests to us a being which is everywhere fleeing, and yet is everywhere similar to itself, which on all sides escapes, yet on which one can float, a being without danger and without memory, which is eternally changed into itself, on which one leaves no mark, and which could not leave a mark on us . . . a being which is eternity and infinite temporality, because it is a perpetual change without anything which changes, a being which best symbolizes . . . a possible fusion of the For-itself as pure temporality, with the In-itself as pure eternity. But immediately the viscous reveals itself as essentially ambiguous, because its fluidity exists in slow motion. There is a sticky thickness in its liquidity; it represents in itself a dawning triumph of the solid over the liquid . . . that is, a tendency of the indifferent In-itself, which is represented by the pure solid [we are reminded of the quality of *being massif* which characterizes the in-itself], to solidify the liquidity, to absorb the For-itself which ought to dissolve it. Viscosity is the agony of water. . . . Nothing testifies more clearly to its ambiguous character . . . than the slowness with which the viscous melts into itself. A drop of water touching the surface of a large body of water is instantly transformed into the body of water. But . . . the honey which slides off my spoon on to the honey in the jar first sculptures the surface by fastening itself on it in relief, and its fusion with the whole is presented as a gradual sinking. . . . In the viscous substance which dissolves into itself there is a visible resistance, like the refusal of an individual who does not want to be annihilated in the whole of being, and at the same time a softness pushed to its ultimate limit. . . . The slowness of the disappearance of the viscous drop in the bosom of the whole is grasped first in the softness, which is like a retarded annihilation and seems to be playing for time, but this softness lasts up to the end; the drop is sucked into the body of the viscous substance. . . . We have here the image of destruction-creation. The viscous is docile. Only at the very moment when I believe that I possess it, behold, by a curious reversal it possesses me. Here appears its essential character: its softness is leech-like. If an object which I hold in my hands is solid I can let it go when I please; its inertia symbolizes for me my total power; I give it its foundation, but it does not furnish any foundation for me. The For-itself should absorb the In-itself. Yet here is the viscous reversing the terms; the For-itself is suddenly compromised. I open my hands, I want to get rid of the viscous and it sticks to me, it draws me, it sucks at me. . . . There is something like a tactile fascination in the viscous. I am no longer the master in checking the appropriation. It continues. In one sense it is like the supreme docility of the possessed, the fidelity of the dog who *gives himself* even when one does not want him any longer; and in another sense there is underneath this docility a surreptitious appropriation of the possessor by the possessed. Here we can see the symbol which abruptly discloses itself: there exists a poisonous possession;

there is the possibility that the In-itself might absorb
the For-itself. . . . At this instant I suddenly understand the snare of the viscous . . . I cannot slide on this
viscosity, all its suction cups hold me back; it cannot
slide over me, it clings to me like a leech. The sliding,
however, is not simply denied as in the case of a solid,
it is degraded. . . . The viscous is like a liquid seen in a
nightmare, where all its properties are animated by a
sort of life, and turn back against me. Viscosity is the
revenge of the In-itself. A sickly sweet, feminine
revenge which will be symbolized on another level by
the quality 'sugary'. This is why the sugar-like sweetness to the taste . . . an indelible sweetness which
remains indefinitely in the mouth, even after swallow-
ing . . . perfectly completes the essence of the viscous.
A sugary viscosity is the ideal of the viscous; it symbolizes the sugary death of the For-itself (like that of
the wasp which sinks into the jam and drowns in it). . . .
To touch the viscous is to risk being dissolved in
viscosity. Now this dissolution by itself is frightening
enough, because it is the absorption of the For-itself
by the In-itself, as ink is absorbed by the blotter. But
it is still more frightening in that the metamorphosis is
not just into a thing but into the viscous. . . . The
viscous offers a horrible image; it is horrible in itself
for a consciousness to become viscous. . . . A consciousness which became viscous would be transformed by
the thick stickiness of its ideas. From the time of our
upsurge into the world we are haunted by the image of
a consciousness which would like to launch forth into
the future, towards a projection of itself, and which at
the very moment when it was conscious of arriving
there would be held back slyly by the invisible suction
of the past and which would have to assist in its own
slow dissolution in this past which it was fleeing. . . .
This is the fear not of death, not of pure In-itself; not
of nothingness, but of a particular type of being. It is
an ideal being which I reject with all my strength, and

which haunts me as value haunts my being, an ideal being in which the foundationless In-itself has priority over the For-itself. We shall call it an anti-value.

Thus Sartre argues that viscosity reveals itself naturally and inevitably as the symbol of an 'anti-value'—of all that we must hate and from which we cannot entirely escape, since the fear of this kind of degeneration of consciousness haunts all our conscious projects. So when in fact we, like Roquentin, suddenly see things as nauseating, we are unable to escape this nausea because in a perfectly good sense we are seeing things as they really are, as thick, clinging, and evasive. When I first meet with something viscous I am presented with a genuine pattern in things, something which will explain in general what the universe is like, what my place in it is, and what my aims are. 'The category [of the viscous] arises like an empty skeletal framework, before any experience with different kinds of viscosity. I have projected it into the world by my original project, when first faced with the viscous. It is an objective structure of the world, and at the same time an anti-value.' From the first moment of my contact with the viscous, the distinction between things and meanings of things is destroyed. I immediately apprehend it as full of meanings which go beyond its actual appearance in the particular case. This is what it is for the viscous to be a natural symbol.

It is not at all difficult to understand what Sartre means by a thing's being a natural symbol. There are many things, especially perhaps natural phenomena, like the sea, or trees, which seem to us immediately to signify something, and about which it would be very reasonable to say that the distinction between the thing and its meanings disappears. It is not just that literature has grown up round such objects, which explains our feelings about them; on the contrary, the feelings are common, and doubtless come first, and explain the literature. What is unusual, and less acceptable, in Sartre's theory is his selection of the viscous as one, and a particularly important one, among these natural symbols. It is hard not to conclude here that his choice is too idiosyncratic to have much general value, and that it must be an exceedingly dubious foundation for a total account of the world. And when one considers the feeling, nausea, which is particularly closely associated with viscosity in his account, and remembers that it is this feeling which must mediate for us, according to him, *all* our awareness of the physical world, then one is most strongly tempted to write the whole thing off as an obsession, or a reflection of some feature of Sartre's own life which one may feel very thankful not to share. And this tendency is not without importance. For it is a weakness of metaphysical description in general that it may or may not *appeal* to us. If it does appeal to us we may think 'this is really how things are'; but if it does not, we may simply wonder dispassionately why these particular categories were chosen as specially noteworthy, and we may be inclined (as people have been with Berkeley, for instance) to give up taking his words seriously, and instead to treat them merely as symptoms of his psychic or indeed of his physical state.

But we should not write off such a description without at least trying to understand its significance for Sartre himself. We need not cease to feel sorry for him for constantly feeling sick; but we should also see how deeply this feeling is woven into the substance of everything that he says about the world. For we come into being as Beings-in-the world. There is no such thing as a person in isolation. Therefore it is absolutely necessary, if we are to understand what consciousness is, to see it as occupying a certain position among things in the world. This cannot be understood unless the necessary attitude of consciousness to its environment is understood. Sartre is never at any time concerned with pure epistemology. There are too many ways of knowing the world for epistemology ever, for him, to be a pure subject. And one of the ways of coming to know the world is to feel emotions in the face of it. Another is to desire to possess it, or to become like it. One of our ways of controlling and possessing the world is to describe it, to give everything its right name. That this is a very deep-rooted desire seems to me self-evident. It is not just a matter of convenience, but of power. It is the desire expressed, for example, by Lara in *Dr Zhivago* when, in a moment of great elation, she said that her role in life was to give names to everything, or, if she could not do it herself, to have children who would do it instead.

We are unable completely to pin down other people by names and labels since they are free and without essence and so they escape us, though this offends us (a grocer who dreams is offensive to the customer, Sartre said). But we are more hopeful that we can pin down material objects; we can state their essences and categorize them, more or less successfully. This is to treat material objects as essentially such that one can generalize about them. There will always be types, kinds, classes, and regular species; so we can plan our life, thinking of some things as 'useful', others as 'dangerous', and so on. Things in this way become parts of our 'hodological map' by which we distinguish means to our own freely chosen ends.

Sartre thought that we naturally want to control things and possess them as well as we can. Simone de Beauvoir records a quarrel which she and Sartre had about this, sitting in a café near Euston station. Sartre had tried to define London as a whole. She objected to his attempt, not only because she thought he had got it wrong and left out a great deal, but because she maintained it was in principle ridiculous to try to sum up reality in a definition. 'I maintained that reality goes far beyond anything we can say about it and that we should face it in all its ambiguity and opacity instead of reducing it to the kind of meaning that can be expressed in words. Sartre replied that if one wished, as one did, to possess reality, it was not enough merely to observe or be touched by things. One must grasp their significance, and pin it down in language.' But in a way he would admit that Simone de Beauvoir was right. There is an aspect even of material objects which makes them recalcitrant; and this is their particularity. If you consider an object by itself, its texture, colour, smell, and so on, you may suddenly cease to be able to think of it as a member of a class; you may even momentarily forget what on earth it is. And the moment you concentrate in this way on its particularity, then you lose grip on it; it ceases to be *normal*—just a familiar thing to be used in the ordinary way. It is then, Sartre says, that one feels nausea. One can no longer be distracted by one's ordinary aims and desires and projects. One is conscious of the world in a new and naked way, as simply possessing certain features which one can in no way control and which may overwhelm one. For in regarding the world in this naked, uncommitted, untidy way there is the fear that one might have to regard oneself in the same way. If I suddenly cease to be able to see a hammer, for instance, as just the thing I need to knock a nail in, which I want to do for some very good, statable purpose—if I suddenly see it instead just as a collection of physical properties which I have no reason to expect ever to see conjoined with one another again—then there is the fear that all my plans and projects themselves, as well as the things I had been accustomed to regard as means to their fulfilment, will melt and dissolve, and become indescribable and particular as well. It is this fear, above all, which the 'anti-value' of viscosity stands for; and it is this fear which gives rise to the nausea against which we try to use descriptive language as an antidote.

(5) *The sense of the absurd, and anguish*

The same sudden refusal of things to remain quietly as tools within our grasp, labelled according to their uses and our needs, gives rise to the closely related feeling of futility or of being *de trop*, superfluous. Nothing is superfluous if it is part of a rational plan. A car, let us say, which stands in front of one's house, is not *de trop* or pointless, so long as one regards it as an essential part of every project one has: one can't get anywhere without it, one may think, and one stops looking at it or considering it as a particular thing; it is just one's car, a necessary condition of one's living as one does; and if one didn't have *this* car, one would have another. So it is completely described by having its make, registration number, and so on listed. There is no more to it than that. But it is possible to regard it as just a physical object; and regarding it in this light would go along with losing interest in one's plans and therefore in all means to their fulfilment. The car becomes pointless—just an object, which might just as well not be there.

Sartre connects the realization of pointlessness or absurdity with the realization by each of us of his own 'facticity', that is to say of the particular contingent facts which are true of each one of us. There is a number of propositions which each of us can state about himself, which are true of him, and which will always be true, facts about his parents, his background, the shape of his nose, the colour of his hair, and so on; and these seem, in a way, a necessary part of each of us. Yet it is also true that a different lot of features could have been, but are not, a part of each of us. All that is necessary is that we should each have *some* given and unalterable features. There is absolutely no reason that can possibly be given why we have those that we have rather than some others. There is no *point* at all in our being as we are. 'I cannot doubt that I am. But in so far as *this* For-itself as such could also not be, it has all the contingency of a fact. Just as my nihilating freedom is apprehended in anguish, so the For-itself is conscious of its facticity. It has the feeling of its complete gratuitousness; it apprehends itself as being there for nothing, as being *de trop*.'

In this passage Sartre explicitly connects the sense of being *de trop* with the anguish in which we realize our freedom. And they are connected in another way: if we might have been different, then so might our values. What we value is a wholly contingent matter, and to pretend otherwise is a version of Bad Faith; it is a denial of our freedom. For in fact we freely choose what projects to hold as important, what to take as ends, what as means to these ends, and what to consider as ultimate values. The claim that there are absolute values (a claim which shows the spirit of Seriousness) is an act of Bad Faith. Anyone who thinks that the path of duty is mapped out before him; that there are actions waiting for him to do; that there are absolute moral laws binding on all men alike whether they recognize them or not—anyone who thinks this is denying his own freedom, and at the same time his own absurdity. He is giving himself a role in life, a function or a mission, whereas in fact he has none. None of us has. Human life is absurd, in that there can be no final justification for our projects. Everyone is *de trop*; everything is dispensable.

Thus both anguish and the sense of absurdity are experienced by us when we consider the contingency of our situation in the world. And we may come to realize this contingency if we contemplate the actual characteristics of the world—if we see it, that is, as made up of a great number of unrelated particular things, with only one common feature, namely that they all of them elude us. It is the actual unmanageableness of things, our failure wholly to possess them, which is the origin not only of nausea but of anguish and the sense of the absurd as well. How these last bear upon our actual conduct, and also upon the question how we *ought* to behave, will be the subject of the next two chapters.

5

Freedom

(1) The paradox of free will

In Part 4 it was shown that, in Sartre's view, our existence in the world is not a matter of knowing the world only, nor even of knowledge combined with action; it is also a matter of feeling and attitude. We must necessarily experience a feeling of nausea when we allow ourselves fully to concentrate on the material substance of the world. We must also, in view of our position in the world, experience the sense of futility and dispensability—the sense of the absurd. And, finally, when we recognize our own freedom we must experience anguish. The question remains, however, to what extent we *are* free. What are we really free to choose? And if we are to any degree free to make choices, does it make sense to say that we ought to choose one thing rather than another? Are some choices better and others worse? In this chapter we must attempt to find out Sartre's answer to these questions. For in his answers lies the chief *message*, if we may so call it, of his existentialist philosophy.

We are faced once again, as we were at the beginning of the last chapter, with a paradox, this time a paradox of a kind painfully familiar to philosophers. Sartre appears to be committed to two incompatible views. On the one hand, he holds that we truly apprehend our own impotence and futility, for we are just parts of the natural world and there is no *point or purpose* in anything in nature. We are born in a certain place at a certain time with certain characteristics which are not of our choosing; and we are committed to

living as we do by all these factors, which are built into us
and are beyond our control. Further, merely by being
human we are, as we have seen, committed to certain views,
desires, and attitudes, just in virtue of being conscious in the
midst of unconscious things in the world, and being there
with, and in conflict with, other conscious beings. The
human position gives rise to many of our thoughts and
attitudes, necessarily. On the other hand, the essence of
consciousness is that it has no essence—that it is empty,
and constructed out of nothing except plans and projects
and attempts of its own devising. There is a gap between
consciousness and the world of things, which consciousness
seeks to fill; and a conscious being *can* fill it however he
chooses to, by actions, and by seeking to possess himself of
the world. We are free to be what we choose to be, and
there is nothing else which we are. Even our feelings, as
much as our actions, are freely chosen, for they are themselves attempts upon the world, just as actions are.

So Sartre seems to face an acute version of the familiar
paradox that human beings are both free and not free. What
does a philosopher do next? Does he distinguish between
the phenomenal and the noumenal worlds? Does he try to
reconcile what is free with what is determined, by showing
that the apparent opposition between them is a false one?
Sartre certainly fails to solve his form of the problem
completely satisfactorily. His conclusion, however, is that
we *are* free, and that we prove it by actually choosing and
acting and planning in a way that no unfree object can.
The difference between the active and the passive, between
doing things and having things happen to one, is a manifest
difference, which can be experienced all the time. Freedom
is the power to do things, and this is part of consciousness;
and so the distinction between the conscious and the
unconscious, between the For-itself and the In-itself, is in
fact identical with the distinction between the free and the
determined. Our 'facticity'—that is, the contingent set of
circumstances which, though contingent, appear to bind us
necessarily to do or be this rather than that—is a basis

upon which we build our free choices, or, better, it is the material out of which our free choices are built. If we fully recognize our freedom we shall recognize that though there may be some things which we physically cannot do, yet we are still free to live with these restrictions in one way rather than another; and we shall realize also that there is nothing to commit us to choosing one way rather than another.

'Facticity' gives us the sense of the absurd, for we see that there is no point in our being as we are. We must have some determining characteristics or other; but, so far as we are determined at all, we are not determined in any particular way. There is, necessarily, *some* limit to our choices, but no particular or *specific* limit. And there could not possibly be any explanation of why my choices are limited as they are, and yours as yours are.

There are two ways of denying one's freedom. One is to insist on thinking of oneself as nothing but facticity—as a part of the material world, stuck down, as a mountain or a tree may be, with the characteristics that one has and the sphere of actions that one happens to find. Another way of denying freedom is to regard oneself as bound by given *purposes*. For instance one might regard oneself as one of God's children, and therefore as bound to behave in the way in which God ordained that one should, or at least in the way of which he approves. Recognizing one's facticity, and thus having a sense of the absurdity of life, makes it impossible to take this refuge from one's own freedom. The other refuge is closed by the facts, as Sartre sees them, of my undeniable power to choose in what way I 'live' my own circumstances—to manage them and even to react to them as I choose.

This, then, is the general picture. We must now take a closer look at the details. Then we shall be in a position to consider what effect his picture of our life and freedom has on Sartre's view of morality.

(2) Human action

It is necessary for a start to go back to the nature of the For-itself, and, in particular, to the question of what constitutes human action. Action, as opposed to mere happening, entails intention. For a human being to act he must have a motive, and this motive must be a thought about the situation in which he finds himself, combined with a thought about the future. It is a necessary part of the For-itself, as we have seen, to be able to conceive the future negatively, as filled with situations which are not yet actual. To conceive a project for the future, or form an intention, is to think of something which is not yet so, but which may be so. This is the power of negation which forms the gap between human beings and the world, the gap which it is their nature to fill in with deliberately chosen actions. But it would be impossible for them to do this if they could not frame judgments of their situation; for they have to judge it in order to alter it, or to alter themselves to fit it. Consciousness must always be consciousness of the world from the point of view of a potential *agent*, of someone who is prepared to act upon his environment. There is no such thing as bare consciousness without connexion with action. It is in this way that freedom, which is built in, as we have seen, to the concept of action, is a necessary part of the concept of consciousness as well. Without consciousness as consciousness of *something to be done*, there would be no action, since there would be no motive.

A state of affairs cannot be a motive; only the awareness of a state of affairs as something to be changed can be. For example, if I am very cold it might be thought that the cold was my motive for getting up to put more on the fire. But the cold itself cannot lead me to any action at all, only to a passive acceptance of it. What constitutes my motive for acting is my apprehension of the cold as something to be overcome, as something which I can change, and as something which in the future does not necessarily persist. I see it, that is to say, as something I can 'do something about'. There are numerous features of our environment about which we think we can do nothing, and so long as we so regard them, they never become a motive for action. Sartre, somewhat wildly, interprets Spinoza's dictum *'omnis determinatio est negatio'* as a confirmation of this view. But, as usual, it is best illustrated by examples.

However, before discussing the examples it will be worth while to quote a little of what he says in general about free action. These quotations come from the first chapter of Part IV of *Being and Nothingness*, which is entitled 'Being and Doing: Freedom'. He says: 'If there is no act without a cause (as the determinists say), this is not in the sense that we can say that there is no phenomenon without a cause. In order to be a cause, the cause must be experienced as such. Of course it does not mean that it is to be thematically conceived and made explicit as in the case of deliberation. But at the very least it means that the For-itself must confer on it its value as cause or motive.'

It is important to notice that Sartre thinks of 'cause' and 'motive' as the same; and that he is prepared to distinguish between conceiving the motive consciously, as in deliberation, and merely conferring its value as cause or motive upon it. We shall return to this distinction, which is far from clear; for one of the main difficulties in understanding Sartre's theory of human action is to make out where he wishes to say that we are responsible for our motives and where he does not. He certainly thinks, as this passage and others show, that we confer certain values upon things, thus making them into motives. But do we necessarily know that we are doing this? Could we do otherwise? If we attempt to assign responsibility to people for what they do, if we ever wish to praise or blame them, or wish that they were otherwise or urge them to improve, then it is essential that we should have some theoretical notion of what they are and are not capable of choosing.

Sartre is aware, in a way, of the necessity for making this theoretical point clear; but it will be seen, I think, that

he does not entirely succeed in doing it. When he discusses
the motive, in this passage, he defines it in terms of the end or
intention of the act, but does not say definitely whether or
not he thinks that the end must be in some way consciously
or knowingly envisaged by the agent. He says: 'The motive
is understood only by the end, that is by the non-existent.
It is therefore in itself a negation. If I accept a niggardly
salary it is doubtless because of fear; and fear is a motive.
But it is fear of *dying from starvation*; that is, this fear has
meaning only outside itself, in an end ideally posited, which
is the preservation of life which I apprehend as 'in danger'.
And this fear is understood in turn only in relation to the
value which I implicitly give to this life; that is, it is referred
to the hierarchical system of ideal objects which are values.
Thus the motive makes itself understood as what it is by
means of the ensemble of beings which "are not", by ideal
existences, and by the future.'

It will be seen how deeply the idea of values is woven
into Sartre's idea of free action—that is of intentional
action. And this connexion is important and useful. Indeed
some of the difficulties about the extent to which Sartre
thinks that we always know what we are choosing, and
what we are choosing it for, may be at least partially avoided
by concentrating on the idea of what we value, rather than
of what we choose. For in a way it would be reasonable to
say that we do and we don't know what our hierarchy of
values is. What we value is demonstrated by how we behave;
but it is not impossible that we should also be able to state
what we value more highly than what, and why we do so.
Do we deliberately choose what we value most highly? It
looks as if the answer might be that we do, or can, choose;
that we need not value what we do, and could value something else more highly; but that we seldom deliberate
about what to value most highly, and that we may not
know what we value until we are called on to prove it in
action. And this is very like what Sartre is saying about
the choice of motives. We look at things in one way rather
than another; we could look at things differently, and we

could even decide to do so, but we seldom deliberate about how to look at things. But it is from our way of looking at things that our motives and thence our deliberate actions arise. Our actions both arise from and reveal our motives.

(3) Motives

Sartre takes examples from history to illustrate the way in which motives arise out of situations. There are two ways of being aware of something: one may have something before one in one's non-reflective consciousness. In this case one will be aware of it without contemplating it. Or one may detach oneself from it and think about it. And only in this case can one form projects in the light of one's experience, and thus turn one's present experience into a motive for deliberate action. For instance, there is a marked contrast in some of Sartre's examples between the mere riot, into which workers might be led without thinking and which would lead to no serious consequences, and the revolution, which must be planned and must arise out of education and detached reflection.

The other point upon which Sartre insists is that the past in itself cannot force a man to act. The situation alone does not cause the revolution; it is the situation regarded as unbearable which causes it—that is, which becomes its motive. 'It is by a pure wrenching away from himself and the world that the worker can posit his suffering as unbearable suffering and consequently can *make of it the motive* for revolutionary action. This implies for consciousness the permanent possibility of effecting a rupture with its own past, so as to be able to consider it in the light of a non-being and so as to be able to confer on it the meaning which *it has* in terms of the project of a meaning which *it does not have*. Under no circumstances can the past in any way by itself produce an act. In fact as soon as we attribute to consciousness this negative power with respect to the world and itself, as soon as the nihilation forms an integral part of positing an end, we must recognize that the indispensable and fundamental condition of all action is the freedom of the acting being.'

(4) Sartre's solution to the free will paradox

This, then, is how Sartre attempts to settle the dispute between determinists and libertarians. Actions do have causes, but they are causes of a peculiar kind; and there could be no such thing as action at all if human consciousness were not free—free to contemplate its situation and to form negative judgments about it and about the future.

There are numerous objections which could be raised against this theory. For one thing it cannot possibly be a sufficient answer to determinism simply to concede that human actions are caused, but in a different way. It does nothing to strengthen such an answer to refer to motives as causes, as Sartre does. The determinist may still argue that causes could be found to explain a man's acting on one motive rather than another. He would not deny what Sartre asserts, namely that one has to have a motive in order to act; he would simply say that to state the motive was not to explain the action completely.

Secondly, it might be objected that Sartre has, by including the notion of freedom in that of action, merely made it a matter of definition that human action is free. And, of course, one may do this if one chooses. But that cannot possibly silence the determinist, who would only shift his position to that of denying that we ever *act*, in the new sense in which actions are necessarily free. There is no reason why the determinist should not deny that we act, as a way of denying that the will is free. The onus might be thought still to rest with Sartre of proving that action in his sense does occur. But as a matter of fact Sartre would not shrink from this. He would deny that what he says about action is *merely* a matter of definition. Though freedom is part of the meaning of action, this is so only *because* freedom is a condition without which action cannot take place. And that it is such a condition is, he would maintain, a matter of experience.

We experience our relation with the outside world as part of the experience of our own being. We should not be aware of ourselves as conscious beings if we were not able at the same time to become aware of the emptiness within us, by which we can think of things which do not yet exist, and because of which, therefore, we can value both these ideal non-existent things and those things which do exist in the present. To arrive at the conclusion that this is what we do is merely to analyse our actual experience. It is not just that when we choose to act we *feel as if* we were free—a point which many philosophers have made (and have variously commented on, whether by saying that the feeling is an illusion, or that it is well founded). Sartre is not relying, he would claim, on a mere feeling. It is rather that we *know* we must be free, if we are conscious at all; and we cannot but know that we are conscious. So Sartre once again is in effect asking a Kantian kind of question, this time 'How is action possible?'; where action means what we all know that it means, namely, doing things rather than having them happen to us. And the answer which he gives is that action is possible only because it arises out of the human capacity to form negative judgments, to deny, and to see how things are not, and that this capacity is identical with freedom. So the question which we noticed earlier, namely, 'How is Bad Faith possible?', is answered in the same way as the present question. It turns out indeed to be merely a more specific form of the question about human action in general; and the answer is, that if people were not free, they could not be as we in fact know that they are—capable of initiating things, and also of pretending and evading things.

(5) Our responsibility for our characters

With this conclusion, that man is free and must necessarily be so, goes Sartre's total rejection of the view that we are determined by the past. But once again we can imagine someone's objecting that Sartre is exaggerating our independence of the past. For even if we cannot be *forced* to do one thing rather than another by what has happened to us in the past, yet surely our characters are formed by what happens to us, and we act in character, and could not, perhaps, at any time choose what characters to have.

It is just this determination through character that Sartre would most emphatically deny. For he holds the austere, and partially Aristotelian, view that we choose not only our actions but our characters as well. And it is at this point in particular that he differs from Freud. His general thesis, as we have seen, is that the material circumstances in which we find ourselves, and for which doubtless, as a rule, we are not, or not directly, responsible, are just the necessary materials out of which we frame our free choices. We may be forced by circumstances to live, let us say, by the sea. But *how* we live there, how we experience the sea, how we allow it to influence our daily life and even the language and the images we most naturally use—all this is something that is in our own power; and as one person differs from another in just these matters, so we can see them deciding differently about how to fill up the vacancy within them, and what 'essential being' to give themselves.

His own account of our responsibility for our own characters is worked out by means of a long example, part of which I shall quote; it is by means of the same example that he most clearly opposes himself to Freud. In elaborating his example Sartre is specifically answering an objection. He has rejected not only the view that my actions arise out of my circumstances and my past, but also the opposite view that they are totally random and unpredictable (not that anyone could very seriously hold this view).

The objector is supposed to ask: 'If my act can be understood neither in terms of the state of the world, nor in terms of the ensemble of my past taken as an irremediable thing, how could it possibly be anything but gratuitous?' To this Sartre replies as follows:

A choice is said to be free if it is such that it could have been other than it is. I start out on a hike with friends. At the end of several hours' walking my fatigue increases and finally becomes very painful. At first I resist and then suddenly I let myself go. I throw my knapsack down on the side of the road, and let myself fall beside it. Someone will reproach me for my act, and will mean thereby that I was free—that is, not only was my act not determined by any thing or person, but also I could have succeeded in resisting my fatigue longer. I could have done as my companions did, and reached the resting place before relaxing. I shall defend myself by saying that I was *too tired*. Who is right? Or, rather, is the debate not based on incorrect premises? There is no doubt that I could have done otherwise, but that is not the problem. It ought to be formulated rather like this: could I have done otherwise without perceptibly modifying the totality of projects which I am; or is the fact of resisting my fatigue such that . . . it could be effected only by means of a radical transformation of my being-in-the world . . . a transformation which is *possible*? In other words I could have done otherwise. Agreed. But at what price?

Sartre goes on to explain that, in his view, fatigue is a mode of consciousness of the world.

Being conscious, I am necessarily aware in a non-reflective way not only of my surroundings, but also of my body, simply because it is with my eyes that I see, with my legs that I climb the hills, and so on. My fatigue then is that which makes me see the hills as interminable or too steep, and feel the sun as too hot. I simply see the world in this way and do not reflect on my tiredness. But there comes a moment when there is a way in which I do seek to become reflectively aware of the tiredness itself; I do not contemplate it

from a distance, but I suffer it. 'A reflective consciousness is directed upon my fatigue in order to live it,
and confer on it a value and a practical relation to
myself.'

It is only when I come to view it in this light that I
think of my fatigue as either bearable or unbearable.
Up to this point I had just been bearing it, or rather
living it. But the fatigue is not a separate thing on its
own; it is not like a heavy load which I can or cannot
carry. It is just an aspect of me; as I become self-
conscious, I regard what I am suffering as bearable or
unbearable. 'At this point the essential question is
raised: my companions are in good health, like me. . . .
They are, for all practical purposes, as fatigued as I
am. How does it happen, therefore, that they suffer
their fatigue differently? Someone will say that the
difference arises from the fact that I am a "sissy" and
they are not . . . but such an evaluation cannot satisfy
us here. We have seen that to be ambitious is to form
the project of conquering a throne or honours. It is
not a given which would incite one to conquest; it is
this conquest itself. Similarly to be a sissy is . . . only a
name given to the way I suffer my fatigue. If therefore
I wish to understand under what conditions I can suffer
a fatigue as unbearable, it will not help to address
myself to so-called factual givens, which are revealed as
being only a choice; it is necessary to attempt to
examine this choice itself and to see whether it is not
explained within the perspective of a larger choice,
within which it would be integrated as a secondary
structure.

The so-called factual given, my character of being a
sissy, is revealed as itself a choice. My companions,
who are also tired, feel their tiredness as if it were a
hot bath, as something they love, and wish to give
themselves up to. They regard this tiredness as a
desirable and enjoyable way of experiencing, and
indeed of possessing, nature. He (my companion) lives

his fatigue in a vaster project of a trusting abandon to nature, of a passion consented to, in order that it may exist at full strength. . . . It is only in and through this project that the fatigue will be able to be understood, and that it will have meaning for him.'

And even this general project of possessing his natural surroundings is itself only a part of a still more general form of life; for abandonment to any physical experience, to warmth, to tiredness, to hunger, to relaxation, all these kinds of abandonment are ways of attempting to be entirely body; and this is a way of trying to bridge the unbridgeable gap between a conscious For-itself and a being In-itself, a solid *massif* being which is through and through whatever it is. So enjoyment of being tired is like any other enjoyment of physical pleasure. It is a way of integrating a consciousness with the enviable world of things. In himself as portrayed in the example, on the other hand, he detects, by applying the same method of analysis, a determination to have nothing to do with his own body, not to take it into account; and this will lead to his tiredness, instead of being suffered flexibly, being grasped firmly 'as an importunate phenomenon which I want to get rid of'—and this simply because my tiredness is the most manifest feature of my actually being here and now in the world. And in contrast with the man who wants to be even more in the world, like an inanimate object, this man who hates his tiredness wants not to be part of the contingent world of things at all, but to be nothing except an object-for-others —something presented for their look and their appraisal, a part of *their* life, so to speak, and not of his own.

Now the method of analysis which Sartre employed to reach the explanation he wanted of the difference between himself and his companions is, he admits, very sketchy and defective so far. But he tries to give some general account of it. He says: 'The problem is to disentangle the *meanings implied* in an act . . . and to proceed from there to richer and more profound meanings, until we encounter a meaning which does not imply any other meaning, and which refers only to itself.' At this point Sartre makes quite clear the difference between his method of analysis and Freud's. He says: 'For Freud, as for us, an act cannot be limited to itself; it refers immediately to more profound structures. And psycho-analysis is the method which enables us to make these structures explicit. Freud, like us, asks: under what conditions is it possible that this particular person has performed this particular act? Like us he refuses to interpret the action by the antecedent moment. The act appears to him symbolic; that is, it seems to him to express a more profound desire which itself could be interpreted only in terms of the initial determination of the subject's libido.' But it is at that point that Sartre dissents. For, he says, in Freud's view it is external circumstances and the history of the subject which determine whether this or that desire shall be acted upon. The agent acts as he does because of factors in his history which determine him to do so, and he is not able himself to tell what the meaning of his acts is, until they are afterwards interpreted for him by his analyst. 'Consequently the dimension of the future does not exist for psycho-analysis. Human reality . . . must be interpreted solely by a return to the past from the standpoint of the present. . . . No pre-ontological comprehension of the meaning of his acts is granted to the subject. And this is just, since in spite of everything his acts are only a result of the past, which is in principle out of reach.' 'If', Sartre continues, 'we accept the method of psycho-analysis we must apply it in a reverse direction.'

Reverting to the particular example, he says that the way the tired man suffers his fatigue is not dependent on the steepness of the slope or the heat of the sun. These may go to make up his fatigue, but they do not explain *why* he suffers it in the way he does rather than in some other way. 'That a certain passionate and tense way of struggling against fatigue can express what is called an inferiority complex we shall not deny. But the inferiority complex itself is a projection of my own For-itself in the world, in the presence of the Other. As such . . . it is a way of choosing myself. This inferiority which I struggle against, and which nevertheless I recognize, this I have chosen from the start. . . . It is nothing other than the organized pattern of my failure-behaviour as a projected plan, as a general device of my being, and each attitude of failure is itself transcendence, since each time I go beyond what exists towards my own possibilities. It is impossible seriously to consider the feeling of inferiority without determining it in terms of the future and of my possibilities. Even assertions such as "I am ugly", "I am stupid", are by nature anticipations. We are not dealing here with the pure establishing of my ugliness, but with the apprehending of the coefficient of adversity, which is presented by women, or society, to my enterprises. And this can be discovered only through and in the choice of these enterprises.' I choose to confront the existence of the Other in the world—'that insuperable scandal'—by presenting the Other with the aspect of my failure. In being inferior I am choosing and discovering the world at one and the same time.

Once again, Sartre is aware that he may be thought to be exaggerating. For are there not far more recalcitrant elements in our world than he has allowed for? We cannot choose the colour of our hair, or what height we are, yet these, or people's remarks about them, may be what determine our attitudes. Sartre can say to this only that our *facticity*—the contingent circumstances of our life—are the necessary materials of choice. 'Of course . . . there remains an unnameable and unthinkable residuum which belongs to the In-itself which is being considered, and which is responsible for the fact that, in a world illuminated by our freedom, this particular crag will be more favourable for scaling and that one not. But this residue is far from being originally a limit for freedom; in fact it is thanks to this residue, that is, to the brute In-itself-as-such, that freedom arises as freedom.' It is because there are material objects and material circumstances, real existent things and times and places, that human beings are separated as they are from what they project. 'It is by means of them [that is, of existent things-in-themselves] that freedom is separated from and reunited to the end which it pursues, and which makes known to it what it is. Consequently the resistance which freedom reveals in the existent, far from being a danger to freedom, results only in enabling it to arise as freedom. There can be a free For-itself only as engaged in a resisting world. Outside this engagement the notions of freedom and of determinism or necessity lose all meaning.'

So Sartre claims that when he says we are always free he is saying something which, while necessarily true, can also be experienced in our choices. Even if our choices are entirely restricted—even if we are in prison, for instance—still we may choose how to conceive the possibility of escape or release, and above all we may choose how to evaluate it. This is what Sartre refers to as the For-itself, or consciousness, 'choosing itself'—choosing, that is, with what projects and values to fill up the gap between its present and its future.

(6) The possibility of moral theory

(a) Psycho-analysis

So human beings are necessarily free. How does Sartre think that we ought to use this freedom of choice? What choices ought we to make? Before we can try to answer this question we must look back for a moment to the contradiction or paradox which, as we saw at the beginning of the chapter, faced Sartre when he came to analysing human freedom. For we are now in a position to understand more clearly the form that the contradiction takes for him.

He is committed to the view that there is a total description of the world, within which can be fitted human beings, the For-itself, as well as inanimate things, the In-itself; and that human beings must, of their very nature, strive to overcome their lack of essence, by filling up the void within themselves by plans and projects; also by trying, in so far as they can, to aspire to the condition of things-in-themselves—solid unambiguous things which are, above all, determined in their behaviour by their essential properties. More concretely, human beings must necessarily enter into a certain definite kind of relation to other human beings, namely a relation of conflict. The Other is, for each of us, the enemy, and the danger, and his look freezes us; we direct our behaviour necessarily to trying to get other people to see us in a certain light, and trying to get them to recognize our freedom; while, on the other hand, we wish to regard them as things, and to possess ourselves of them entirely. So all human relations—and especially those, such as love, in which we are most deeply engaged—are bound to be hopeless struggles in which neither side can be satisfied. This is the deduction which Sartre draws from his general ontological description of the world and its contents.

But if we are doomed to these thoughts, these aspirations, and these struggles, and only these, how can we possibly be said to be free? What can be meant by saying that we choose ourselves, or that we choose how to live in our peculiar circumstances and situation, if we are committed, by being human, to a general pattern of behaviour such as Sartre has described? There is no answer to this question. Sartre accuses Freud of denying human freedom by basing his method of analysis of human behaviour on the supposition that we are determined by our past experiences to behave as we do. But his method of analysis, in so far as it has any definite basis at all, must rest on the equally deterministic assumption that we form the projects we do because of our commitment to possess others and the world.

Of course, it may truly be said that absolutely any method of analysis, if it is designed to explain human behaviour in terms other than superficial or common-sense terms, must do so in the light of *some* general theory. This is what such an explanation consists in. And there cannot be a *general* theory of human nature which does not commit its holder to some general views about how human beings necessarily behave. And so from the very outset Sartre, as

well as Freud and any one else who undertakes the task of
analysis, is committed to a certain degree of determinism.
But Freud's position is less precarious than Sartre's, for
two main reasons.

The first, and most obvious, may be thought to be a
merely contingent advantage: Freud's theory, though we
may dissent from it, nevertheless has been shown, to a
certain limited extent, to work. That is, analysis of human
behaviour in accordance with his method has actual results.
It is, as it was meant to be, therapeutic. But it is not clear
whether Sartre's theory could ever be applied, nor whether
it is even meant to be therapeutic. Perhaps it is meant only
to give a *true* account of human motivation. But then there
are obvious practical difficulties in reaching the truth by
his method. For imagine trying to get the man in the
example, who gave up on the walk, to accept the analyst's
account of his behaviour, if the analyst were a Sartrean.
The analyst would try to extract from the man an admission
of what he had in mind, what he planned, at the moment
when he threw down his rucksack. But he might get no
further than the expected answer 'I was too tired to go
on'. This would, on Sartre's theory, be an answer in Bad
Faith; and if the man had expressed regret that he could
not go on, this would have been further Bad Faith, since
the solution is to be that he *wants* to fail. And since Sartre
has totally rejected, as itself a creation of Bad Faith, the
notion of the unconscious, he cannot fall back on the
explanation that unconsciously the man wants to fail. He
is bound to think that sooner or later by questioning the
man will be got to agree that, at a conscious level, he
really wanted to fail. And this, one can't help feeling, may
never happen.

Now it is clear that the Freudian analyst also may come
up against every kind of resistance or ignorance, or lack of
belief that any further account of his action is needed
beyond the immediate one. But he can at least take certain
empirical steps. He can try to find out what has happened
to the man already. The defect of Sartre's proposal to

analyse human conduct not in terms of the past, but of the future, is that, except for a crystal-gazer, it is impossible to do this. It may very well be true, and it certainly has great plausibility, to say that a man cannot be cured of his manifestations of inferiority, such as giving things up easily, or stammering, without changing his whole 'project of himself upon the world'. But the difficulty seems to be that Sartre offers us neither the means of finding out what his present project is, nor of bringing him to accept a different one.

Sartre's insistence that the future, and only the future, holds the clue to the patient's condition looks like a conscious paradox, a kind of doctrinaire hostility to Freud. It is perhaps relevant to remind ourselves of his loathing and hatred of the idea of the 'viscous consciousness'—which, it will be remembered, was constantly sucked back from its free projects of itself upon the world by the cloying, sweetly sticky past. This kind of consciousness was the paradigm of the hateful and the disgusting. It is possible that Sartre has been led to exaggerate the difference between his own kind of analysis and Freud's by a quite personal and private horror of the feebleness and flabbiness which he detects in the attitude of one who would try to shuffle off responsibility by explaining his own conduct in terms of his past history. The viscous consciousness is the consciousness which, in the end, would fail because of its own belief that it was determined.

But these may seem frivolous or ignorant objections. After all, Sartre himself admits that everything still needs to be done to perfect the system of analysis which he would substitute for the Freudian. The other respect, however, in which Freud avoids the difficulties which bedevil Sartre's theory is the negative one that Freud is not especially committed to any view of human freedom. His interest is only in human behaviour, and not at all in metaphysics. He does not *have* to accommodate his account of human behaviour to any particular ontological account of the world in general. Sartre has made his own contradictions, by attempting to *deduce* the correctness of his method of analysis from the truth of his most general metaphysical account of what there is in the world. And there is no doubt that the existence of this giant contradiction at the heart of his description of human freedom inhibits his answer to the question 'What ought we to choose?' For as soon as he starts to consider it he comes up against the obstacle that moral advice is futile if offered to people who are committed in advance to the condition of hopeless strife in which he has placed them.

(b) *Ethics*

There can be no ethical theory which does not have as its first concern the behaviour of human beings towards one another; for morality consists in the regulation of this behaviour. Therefore the problem which Sartre has set himself is to discover a way by which human beings can break out of the pattern of behaviour, the endless frustration, to which he has doomed them when they confront each other. There is a somewhat mysterious hint of how this might be done in a footnote to *Being and Nothingness*. In the discussion of the desire which each one has to possess the Other and treat him as a thing, Sartre has concluded that in all human relations whatsoever one is bound to fall into one or other of the two basic attitudes: sadism or masochism. The For-itself, he says, may try relapsing into hatred of the Other, when his attempts to possess him have failed. But, 'hate does not enable us to get out of the circle. It simply represents the final attempt, the attempt of despair. After the failure of this attempt nothing remains for the For-itself except to re-enter the circle, and allow itself to be indefinitely tossed from one to the other of the two fundamental attitudes.' And this appears to be his last word. But he adds a footnote (p. 412) in which he says: 'These considerations do not rule out the possibility of an ethics of deliverance and salvation. But this can be achieved only after a radical conversion which we cannot discuss here.'

It is plain that the radical conversion must be a change of

E

plan, a new way for each man to project himself on the world, and to envisage his own future and his life with his fellow-humans. But Sartre gives us no idea here what the new way would be. Jeanson, however, in an admirable study *Le problème morale et la pensée de Sartre* (Paris 1947), argues that the conversion referred to in the note is a conversion to Marxism, that is, from the primitive level of individual self-interest to the more sophisticated level of interest in oneself as a member of a group or community. It is virtually certain that he is right, not only because Sartre is known to accept Jeanson's interpretation of his writings in preference to that of any other critic, but also because, in the event, he turns out to have done what Jeanson suggests—that is, to have given up the individual-istic and personal standpoint of *Being and Nothingness* in favour of the Marxist sociological standpoint which he adopts in his last book, *The Critique of Dialectical Reason*. We shall discuss this great change of standpoint in the next chapter.

But however this may be, within the context of *Being and Nothingness* itself the footnote is impossible to under-stand. For though the question whether or not to join the communist party was the major moral decision for Sartre at the time, to join would necessarily be to subscribe to the dogma that some things are right and others wrong, that one has duties lying before one; and to submit, perhaps, one's own personal evaluation of things to the test of a different, or at least a common, standard of values. But to do this would be to succumb to Bad Faith and to the 'spirit of seriousness' against which Sartre is adamant in *Being and Nothingness*. For one of the main conclusions of the whole book is that values are contingent. If anything has value for us, then we have freely chosen to assign that value ourselves. To forget this is to fall into the spirit of seriousness, and a morality based on this is a morality of Bad Faith. 'It has obscured all its goals in order to free itself from anguish. Man pursues being blindly, by hiding from himself the free project which is this pursuit. He makes himself such that he is *waited for* by all the tasks along his way. Objects are mute demands, and he is nothing in himself but the obedience to these demands.' It is not only Marxism which is ruled out by the fear of Bad Faith. A Kantian or a Utilitarian morality would be equally 'serious'; and the most obvious victim of all would be a morality which relied upon there being absolute values in the world, which insisted that there were some things intrinsically good in themselves.

Sartre did indeed make one half-hearted attempt to find a way by which many could be shown to have, and to be right to exploit, some altruistic interest in others. And if he had succeeded, this would at once have been a way out of the perpetual hopeless struggle of each against the other, and therefore a foundation for morality. In an essay entitled *L'existentialisme c'est un humanisme*, published in 1946 and translated more than once into English, he suggested that each of us was interested in his own freedom, but that this necessarily involved the freedom of others. It was impossible, he said, to choose one's own freedom without thereby choosing freedom for others as well. For it would be self-contradictory to desire freedom as an end, without universalizing this end and including in it the freedom of all. Sartre expressly compares this doctrine with Kant's moral theory; and it is clear how it might lead to a positive morality. For not only is one committed by it to treating others as free agents, and as ends in themselves, but also, since freedom in the context of the essay means political and social freedom, a kind of Utilitarian programme of actual social and political reforms could be envisaged as arising out of it —a programme of the kind which Mill would have approved. However, it must be admitted that Sartre provided no arguments to show why choosing freedom for oneself involved choosing it for others; and the whole basis of the discussion of our relation to one another in *Being and Nothingness* was the very opposite belief—namely, that one man's freedom was a hopeless obstacle to another's. Moreover, Sartre himself is known to have regretted the publication of this essay; and in *The Critique of Dialectical Reason* he explicitly repudiates the Kantian view that one can treat others as ends in themselves. So it is not possible, though it might be desirable, to accept the solution offered in the essay as a way out of the dilemma presented by *Being and Nothingness*. The fact is that there is no way out, without the conversion which Sartre hinted at. With the materials here presented, there can be no morality. But Sartre does not say this explicitly.

Let us sum up what we have learned, and see what conclusion he reaches. First of all men are free, and 'freedom is precisely the nothingness which is *made to be* in the heart of man and which forces human reality to make itself instead of to be. . . . For human reality, to be is to choose oneself.' Choosing oneself entails assigning values to things, and this we necessarily do in regarding some goals as worth pursuing. To evaluate something, to say that it is good, is not to describe it: this familiar thought of moral philosophers is familiar to Sartre as well. To say that it is good is to set it up as something to be aimed at; but it is also to assert it as an ideal, and therefore as unattainable. The unattainability of the morally perfect seems to Sartre to provide the reason why moral philosophers have always thought that properties like goodness both existed unconditionally, and also did not exist at all. Arguments about the existence of God also start from this fact. Every human being forms the project of becoming somehow perfect, and thereby losing the essential human characteristic of emptiness and imperfection. 'God' is the name given to the impossible conjunction of properties which we all aim to have, the conjunction of consciousness with solid, *massif* Being-in-itself. 'Every human reality is a passion, in that it projects losing itself so as to found being and at the same stroke to constitute the In-itself which escapes contingency, by being its own foundation, the *ens causa sui* which religions call God. Thus the passion of man is the reverse of that of Christ, for man loses himself as man, in order that God may be born. But the idea of God is contradictory, and we lose ourselves in vain; Man is a useless passion.'

And yet, though Sartre does not show at this point what it could possibly be, that there must be some morality is part of his thesis too. For 'Value is everywhere and no-where; at the heart of the nihilating relation "reflection-reflecting" it is present and out of reach, and it is simply lived, as the concrete meaning of that lack which makes my present being. . . . Thus reflective consciousness can properly be called moral consciousness, since it cannot arise without at the same time disclosing values.' Accepting values from another, indeed accepting any kind of general rules for behaviour, must be Bad Faith. To avoid Bad Faith, everyone must choose himself by himself. This is moral advice, but negative. It is the advice of romanticism, and the heroic desire not to be insincere or phony. But it has no positive content whatever.

How to give it content is once more hinted at, at the very end of *Being and Nothingness*. There Sartre says that once the moral agent has realized that he is himself the source of all values 'his freedom will become conscious of itself and reveal itself in anguish, as the unique source of value, and the emptiness by which the *world* exists'. The possibility of acting must always be realized in the context of the world, and this includes for each of us his situation and the people with whom he is. The question, then, becomes one of trying to discover how far a free agent can escape from his particular situation in his choices; and of how much responsibility he will accept for bringing the world in which he is into being. To these questions Sartre promises to give an answer in a book written 'on an ethical plane'. But in fact, in order to answer them, he had to give up the view that each of us entirely independently forms his own projects. A totally romantic and individualistic morality is a contradiction; morality means the accommodation of one person to the interests of another, and this is exactly what Sartre has ruled out in *Being and Nothingness*, both by suggesting that it is metaphysically impossible for human beings ever to do other than fight each other, and also by the thesis that to accept general rules to bring about the possibility of treating other people as ends in themselves is to fall into Bad Faith. It is not surprising that, finding himself in this impasse, Sartre took a radical way out, and, as we shall see, allowed the individual to be swallowed up in the group, and existentialism thereby to be swallowed up in Marxism.

6

The radical conversion

Critique of Dialectical Reason

Sartre, at the end of *Being and Nothingness*, promised a book on ethics. What he wrote, in fact, was a book on sociology. We have seen what he had to say on psychology, on metaphysics and ontology, and on what looked like the widest subject of all, the general relation between man and the world. But in 1960 came the publication of Volume I of the *Critique de la Raison Dialectique*. And in this huge book of 750 pages, Sartre claims to have taken on a yet more fundamental task, that of providing a rational foundation for *all* future thought about man, a foundation for anthropology. He has succeeded in rendering his thought, and the style of his writing, still more abstract and obscure than it was in *Being and Nothingness*. Whether anything has been gained to compensate for the loss of concreteness and insight is less clear. Indeed it must be admitted that it is a depressing task to analyse this latest book, as much as we have of it; for in it we see the spectacle of the death of Sartrean existentialism. Some may not regret this; but it is impossible not to dislike the manner of its passing, even if it has to die. The book is a monster of unreadability. It may be thought unfair to pass judgment on a book of which only the first half has appeared. But there is plenty in Volume I to give a clear indication of the scope and purpose of the whole. It cannot be understood except as an attempt to justify the conversion hinted at in *Being and Nothingness*. It is a deliberate rejection of the individual.

(1) Dialectical reason

The title, *The Critique of Dialectical Reason*, is Kantian. Kant, in his *Critiques*, aimed at determining what could and what could not be established *a priori*. Thus the *Critique of Pure Reason* claims to provide an *a priori* foundation for scientific thought about the world; the *Critique of Practical Reason* a similar foundation for morals. On this analogy, Sartre claims to provide an *a priori* foundation for 'dialectical thought about man, his history and his future'. But the foundation is supposed to be of a peculiar kind. For, according to Sartre, though the *a priori* truths held by Kant to lie at the root of all thought can in fact be doubted, his own *a priori* truths cannot, since they are, in a unique way, self-verifying. A man could go in for scientific thought while nevertheless dissenting, for example, from the Kantian view that 'Every event has a cause' is a necessary but non-tautologous truth; a man could decide what to do in a given situation while not believing in any categorical imperative. But Sartre's claim is that no one can go in for dialectical thought, without thereby proving, as he does so, the *a priori* truth which lies at the foundation of all such thought.

But here at once we encounter a grave difficulty, which Sartre never really attempts to resolve. Everyone knows what scientific thought is, and what thought about action is, so that, though one may believe that Kant's programme of founding these upon reason is mistaken, or impossible to carry out, still what he proposes to do is intelligible. But what *is* dialectical thought? Do we all indulge in it, and if so, why do we? The first and crucial difference between Kant and Sartre is that Kant, it seems, takes a real philosophical problem, which is truly general, and which arises out of a general and recognizable human activity, and, perhaps rashly, claims to have solved it. Sartre on the other hand appears merely to invent a problem, so that it is difficult to take seriously the question whether he solves it or not. Why bother either to succeed or to fail to give dialectical reason an *a priori* foundation if we never employ dialectical reason anyway?

Perhaps a very brief glance at the history of the word 'dialectic' may help us, as a start, to understand what his project is. Plato used the Greek work διαλεκτική, in the *Republic,* for the particularly splendid kind of thought which only philosophers could practise, and which led those who did practise it finally to the knowledge of reality, which others could acquire only second-hand. Dialectical thought for him was philosophical thought. To practise it was difficult and was a way of life in itself. The goal of such thought was *total* understanding of *everything.*

For Hegel, all thought was dialectical, and the word now came to have the predominant meaning of *proceeding by contradictions,* thesis, antithesis, and synthesis; a meaning which may perhaps have been hinted at in Plato, but not in the Hegelian form. According to the doctrine of the Hegelian dialectic, the aim of *all* thought was, ultimately, to comprehend everything, and thus, in a way, the thinker aimed to *be* everything. For, being an idealist, he held that there were not two worlds, that of thought and that of the objects of thought or things. There was only one, the world of thought. The more men could comprehend, the more nearly they approached to the state of identity with the totality of things, or the absolute. If one aims at more and more knowledge this is to aim to surpass one's present state and *become* the absolute totality of things.

The concept of 'totalization' is central to the dialectic. It is not a matter of generalizing from limited experience so much as of seeing how one truth fits in with the totality of truths. For it is essential, before either the Platonic or the Hegelian dialectic can begin to make sense, to think of the universe as rational, that is as coherent, with every fact ideally deducible from any other. This coherence cannot ever be fully grasped, but the more we know, the nearer we come to the unattainable ideal. So, in the writings of Hegel, dialectic is the name of this progressive thought; it is the name of the process of man's becoming god. For if all the coherences were comprehended man would be the absolute totality of coherent ideas. History is therefore the history of this progressive thought; and history is said to be dialectical, that is to proceed by contradiction and synthesis, because thought is so.

Now Marx, as is well known, turned the Hegelian dialectic on its head. He reintroduced the common-sense distinction between thought and things, but held that thought was dialectical because things, the world, progressed dialectically, and man's thought was a reflection of the world, its movement caused by changes in the world. I shall have more to say about Marx later. For the moment a very crude summary must suffice. He found in history a progress by contradiction and synthesis, and he held that men intervene in the world by taking part, whether they wish to or not, in the struggle, which is not primarily a conflict of ideas, but of economic man against economic man, of class against class.

Sartre believed that Marx discovered this dialectic in the world, empirically; and his claim in the *Critique* is to justify the Marxist writing of history, by showing that there is an absolute necessity which lies at the foundation of all thought about the world, proving that such thought can only be dialectical. He claims to show the necessity of what Marx just took on trust, from experience. The necessity, he claims, is such that one cannot even describe man's place in the world and in world history without *thereby* expressing the necessity of the dialectic. The aim being, as we have seen, to provide a foundation for historical, or more properly anthropological, thought, Sartre argues that it is impossible to undertake such thought *without* proving its necessity, in the act of doing so. For man's action in the world, his work, his rational intention in the material universe, which is called by the Marxist name of 'praxis' —this is itself necessarily dialectical in form. It proceeds by the clash and the overcoming of contradictions.

There is here a kind of echo of *Being and Nothingness*. For there, as we have seen, all thought about the world involved negation. The power men have of holding things at a distance from themselves and realizing that they, the thinkers, are not identical with the object of thought, this power was the 'gap' which was the essence of consciousness. Thought could not occur without it. This negative behaviour, which was there the essential of thought and of freedom itself, has now changed into a clash; not a denial, nor a negation, but a *contradiction*. The connexion between the two is not precisely worked out, but it exists. Indeed, throughout the *Critique*, Sartre never tells us *precisely* what is supposed to contradict what in human 'praxis'—what is the thesis and what the antithesis. We are told that, since human action changes a given state of affairs in the world into another, different, state of affairs, and since a man is responsible for the change, which nevertheless is a change in material not wholly within his control, there is some clash, contradiction, or basic incompatibility between what he plans (which is a mental entity) and what actually turns out to happen (a physical change)—even in the cases where what he does is what he intends to do. For he has imposed something alien upon the material world. The trouble is that we cannot very easily make sense of this supposed contradiction by means of which men operate upon their material environment; it seems difficult, at any rate, to justify using the word 'contradiction'. The idea of the gap in consciousness in *Being and Nothingness* was more or less intelligible; but in its transformed Marxist condition, it hardly seems intelligible at all. The transformation is fundamental to the whole work, but it remains quite unclear. There are many such transformations brought about by the 'radical conversion', as we shall see, but sadly, nearly all of them are changes for the worse, or rather for the more obscure.

In any case, Sartre claims that it is impossible to undertake any rational activity at all, including philosophical and historical research, without being aware that one's activity is dialectic in form. For thought and action are date progressive. We leave one situation behind in our plans, and in accordance with these plans, we move to a new situation, to be itself superseded in turn. The analysis of the concept of 'praxis' will bring with it awareness, by experience, that each individual act is part of this dialectical process. And so the *Critique of Dialectical Reason* will start from experience, but from experience of a peculiar kind— namely, the experience of each individual that he is capable of freely intervening in the world in 'praxis', and that 'praxis' proceeds by means of the dialectical struggle to replace the present by a *foreseen* future. It is thus on the notion of 'praxis' that the whole edifice of the *Critique* rests.

(2) Marxism

We must now look more closely at its construction and contents. In the Preface to the *Critique*, Sartre says that one question is asked, namely, 'Have we the means today of setting up a structural and historical anthropology?' He claims that this is the only question asked in the book, and explains that it is set in the context of Marxist thought because 'Marxism is the inescapable philosophy of our time'. He has extracted, he says, from Hegelian and Marxist thought the basic assumption that both history and thought itself are dialectical in movement, that they work, and are now working, towards totalization or completion. Dialectic, he says, has become self-conscious. More than that, it is simply to be found, observably at work in human affairs. But nevertheless, though dialectic is visibly at work all round us, there is the Kantian question to be asked, 'How is it possible?' Kant had no doubt that we are all of us aware of the reality of the categorical moral imperative; he therefore thought that the philosophical question was not 'Is there a categorical imperative?' but rather (since we know that there is), 'How is it possible?' Similarly Sartre is not calling into question the fact (as he takes it to be) that the movement of history and of thought is dialectical, but is raising the philosophical question of how this is possible.

This comes to the same as asking 'What is the special character of man's reasoning about man?' This reasoning is essentially not theoretical but practical; and so there emerges a new relation between thought and its object—a relation which is both thought about the object and change in the object at the same time. This new relation on which the dialectic rests is, as we have seen, 'praxis'. It is the examination of this that will show how the dialectic is possible: man's thought about himself and his environment is necessarily dialectical. 'Praxis' is the foundation which cannot help proving the existence of the dialectic.

A little more light is thrown on Sartre's intention by the preliminary essay *The Question of Method*, which is printed after the Preface, immediately preceding the *Critique* itself. This essay was first published in 1957, in a Polish periodical, under the title *The Situation of Existentialism in 1957*. It was later altered considerably and it appeared in *Les Temps Modernes* under the title *Existentialisme et Marxisme*. In it, Sartre tries to clarify his own relation to Marxism, and to sketch the way in which he means to wed his existentialist view of the world to the Marxist view.

With regard to his own relation to Marxism, it should be made clear at once that he is at best a very eccentric Marxist. But it does not seem to me to be philosphically interesting to try to decide whether he should be *called* a Marxist or not. This may perhaps be of political interest, but that is another thing. What is certain is that he believes himself to have been converted to some form of Marxism, however broadly interpreted. He maintains that every age has a dominant philosophy, but, in addition, there may be lesser systems, which do not deserve the title of philosophies and which he calls 'ideologies'. These are conceived within the general framework of the dominant philosophy, whether their authors realize this or not. Marxism is without doubt the philosophy of the twentieth century, and existentialism is an ideology conceived within its framework. Sartre makes no greater claim for his view of the world than that it may fertilize Marxism, and may bring fresh life to a system which is temporarily ossified.

It is not entirely clear what Sartre means by 'philosophy'.

His point seems to be that there is not just one system of philosophy which is true once and for all. It is futile to search for any such thing. On the other hand there cannot be more than one philosophy at a time. A philosophy, he says, emerges as that which gives expression to the whole movement of society at a given time. It determines the cultural and all other developments in a society for the time being. So 'a philosophy' is something like a set of presuppositions, shared by members of a given society at a given time. But it may also be a set of theories, in accordance with which actual changes come about. The power to change the world is what characterizes Marxist philosophy. There have been few actual dominant philosophies in the history of mankind. Sartre speaks of the age of Descartes and Locke, the age of Kant and Hegel, and now the age of Marx. Within one of these ages, for instance the present Marxist age, it is impossible to have any philosophical thought which is not either Marxist or a return to some pre-Marxist thought; or, if there is an apparent innovation which seems to go beyond Marxism, this will turn out to be merely an elaboration of something already contained in the system. The thinkers, professional philosophers and others, who work within the systems are like people working some piece of land. They exploit the natural resources, but could do nothing if the land were not rich enough in itself to be exploited. These are the ideologists, among whom Sartre counts himself.

There is surely something mysterious about this notion of dominant philosophies. It is all very well to look back, take an Olympian view of the history of thought, and speak of 'the age of rationalism', 'the age of idealism', and so on. This we frequently do. We may well, however much attention we may pay to the originality of individual philosophers, nevertheless see all eighteenth-century philosophers as set on a certain path by Descartes—separating, perhaps, the contents of consciousness from the external world, interested in problems of knowledge rather than of logic, and so on. But it is almost impossible to take this kind of Olympian view of the age in which one is oneself living; nor is it at all desirable to try to do it. For philosophy has never proceeded except by means of attention to particular problems which have, for the time being, seemed to a particular philosopher obsessively difficult or puzzling. Such actual difficulties cannot possibly be resolved by an appeal to the history of thought, nor by taking stock of the general situation of thought about the subject in question. To confuse philosophy with the history of ideas, or with anthropology, is to kill the subject; and the trouble about this is that, in fact, philosophy is a subject which will not be killed. If one person tries to turn it into anthropology, someone else, perhaps some amateur, or someone engaged in some quite different subject, will raise philosophical questions all over again in some different quarter. However, it is precisely such a reduction of philosophy to something else which Sartre is proposing, when he says that Marxism is for the time being '*indépassable*'.

Let us see how he claims to know that this is so. All we are told about this is that Sartre and his contemporaries at the university were taught by people who had such a horror of the concept of dialectic that Hegel was unknown to them, and Marx was nowhere taught. In ignorance of the dialectic, Sartre read *Das Kapital*, but understood it only academically; that is, reading it made no difference to him. He and his contemporaries wrongly thought that it was possible to study Marx as one might study any other philosophy or sociology. What began to change their minds was not anything that they had read, but what they saw around them. 'It was the reality of Marxism, the heavy presence on my horizon of the mass of workers, a vast sombre body who lived Marxism, who practised it, and who exercised from a distance an irresistible attraction for the bourgeois intellectuals.' Then finally came the war, the occupation, and the resistance. It was this that broke the pattern of their previous ways of thought. Fighting beside the workers, they discovered, Sartre says, that 'the concrete is history, and action is dialectic'.

(3) The contribution of existentialism to Marxism

But though he now deliberately accepted Marxist philosophy, this did not mean entirely giving up his own previous theories. For Marxist theory had come to a stop; it had got stuck in a bog of dogmatism. Sartre treats Marxist concepts as essentially ambiguous, susceptible of numerous different interpretations; they are directive principles, indications of tasks; they set problems, rather than providing actual concrete truths, 'In a word, they appear to us as regulative ideas' (*Question of Method*, p. 33). Contemporary orthodox Marxists, on the other hand, regard the works of Marx and Engels as unambiguous, clear, and giving the whole precise truth. 'For them, they constitute a science already. We think, on the other hand, that everything remains to be done. We must find a method and set up a science.'

Marxist method itself is regarded as unsatisfactory, in that it is unduly *a priori*. Everything that happens is forced into a preconceived mould, the mould of dialectical materialism; and it becomes less and less necessary for Marxists to examine the facts, the more set in their dogmatic preconceptions they become. What Sartre proposed, therefore, was the 'interiorization' of Marxist thought, and the rendering of it concrete.

'Interiorization' seems to mean the same as 'making concrete'. If we remember Sartre's earlier desire for a philosophy of *things*, individual concrete things, this is intelligible. 'Interiorization' means a change from a view from outside, as it were from above, which sees the world of men, animals, artefacts, and landscape are indifferently working in dialectical conflict, to a view which is essentially that of *one* man, looking out from himself, through his own eyes, on the world of others, and of things which are objects *for* him; it is a change to the world seen *from a certain point of view*. Here we see once again the old pull

144

of Cartesianism, or rather of Sartre's version of Descartes. 'Cogito ergo sum', as we have seen, essentially means for Sartre '*I* think'. Interiorization therefore means seeing the dialectical process, and the changes in the world according to this process, from the inside, and from the point of view of the agent.

But, again remembering Sartre's earlier theories, it is possible to see how this entails an increase in concreteness. For there is no such thing as 'human nature' in general. Therefore each agent will see the world his *own* way, and form projects and act according to his *own* decisions. These decisions will be made in the light of the particular situation in which *he* is, surrounded by actual objects and actual people. Thus 'interiorization' leads to discussion of individual action from a particular, not a general, standpoint; and the particular is for Sartre identical with the concrete. By the concrete, indeed, he means the things, whatever they are, which are before me here and now; what I am aware of when I open my eyes—*this* bottle, *this* table, *this* street. So what he proposes is the superficially attractive task of forcing Marxist theory to take account of men, and men in particular concrete situations. The dialectic of history is to be seen and proved through their eyes.

But, of course, Marxism rests specifically upon the concept, not of the individual, but of the class. Sartre claims that existentialism, grafted upon Marxist theory, can show how the notion of the class arises. A man has only to look out of his window to see evidences of 'collectives', or groups, all around him. 'I see a church, a bank, a café. Here are three collectives. This thousand-franc note is another; another again is the newspaper I have just bought.' One of the charges which Sartre levels against Marxism, in its present state, is that it fails to examine these social institutions for their own sake, with all their particular ramifications, and with the particular effect they have as a part of the environment of this individual man and that. 'The child does not see only his family; he also sees, partly through the family and partly by himself, the collective landscape which surrounds him. And it is the generality of his class which is revealed to him in this particular experience.' That is to say, Marxists are reproached for losing sight of all the actual concrete factors which determine man's life. In this way they preserve nothing even of their own concept of the 'totalization' of history, except in so far as it can be fitted into their abstract, diagrammatic view of history and the world.

Marxist theory, by being so determinedly abstract, has reduced history to a fantastically general sketch, within which what actually happened on any given occasion is made to seem a matter of chance. By insisting upon discussing, for instance, the rise of Napoleon in absolutely general terms, they are led to the position of saying that *some* military dictatorship was necessary, but not necessarily *this* one; given similar economic and social conditions, a similar dictatorship would arise again, but with some other dictator. Napoleon himself, therefore, drops out of the account of the dictatorship as an irrelevant accident. 'The result is that they have entirely lost the sense of *what man is*. They have nothing to fill the gaps but an absurd Pavlovian psychology. . . . When someone says "Napoleon, in so far as he was an individual, was nothing but an accident; what was necessary was military dictatorship as the régime to destroy the Revolution", we are not in the least interested, because we have always known it. But what we aim to prove is that *this* Napoleon was necessary, that the development of the Revolution forged at the same time the necessity for a dictatorship *and* for the whole personality of the man who was going to be the dictator; that the process of history allotted to *Bonaparte personally* the powers and the opportunities which enabled him, and him alone, to hasten the end of the Revolution. In short it is not a case of an abstract universal, nor of a situation so ill defined that numbers of Bonapartes were possible, but of a concrete "totalization" in which *this* real bourgeoisie, composed of real living men, had to bring *this* Revolution to an end.' Sartre claims to have found in the centre of Marxist theory an empty place, and it is this empty place which he wishes to fill up with a concrete anthropology. The fundamental concept upon which Sartre relies for the performance of this proposed rejuvenation of Marxism is, once again, that of 'praxis'. This was the concept which was to carry within it the proof of the dialectical movement of world history: it also has to bear the burden of rendering possible the rehumanizing of this dialectic.

(4) *Praxis*

Praxis is, as we have seen, human activity, and the notion of human activity necessarily contains within it two parts. The first is the subjective plan, or project, which a man forms when he thinks of his situation, his purposes and needs. The second is the objectively existing situation in which the man finds himself, and which he plans to change. The essence of praxis is *'dépassement'*—going beyond the existing situation. But this is not possible without the element of intention. It is not necessary that a man should know *exactly* either what he means to do, or even what he is doing, what objective change he is bringing about by his act. But nevertheless he must be aware of something, generally of some need or lack, which makes him think of how things are *not*, and he must be able to *say* what at least he believes that he is doing. It is this ability to imagine that things might be different which makes man capable of praxis, capable of going beyond the particular situation in which he is. It is this, too, which proves that praxis is dialectical in form, for the dialectic is the clash between project and fact. Thus the word 'praxis' means very much the same as it meant for Aristotle, who used it to mark off purposive goal-directed activity from random activity, and who held that children and animals could not be said to go in for praxis, presumably because they could not say what it was that they were doing, or why.

It is, then, impossible, according to Sartre, to make use of the concept of praxis without thereby directing attention first upon the concrete situation in which a man is and with reference to which he forms his projects, and secondly upon the thoughts or projects themselves. It is therefore impossible to regard human behaviour as merely governed by natural laws to be totally explained and understood by an observer watching the behaviour of men as he might watch the behaviour of material objects in certain conditions. Behaviourism is inadequate, and incompatible with the notion of praxis. Human actions must be divided into an inside and an outside—what a man intends, and what he does.

But what he does intend, and how he thinks of his environment, is itself determined by the social setting in which he finds himself. And it is upon this social setting that he then acts, to change it. So man can truly be said to be the product of his own product: but not a *passive* product. 'It is in going beyond the given towards the field of possibilities, and in realizing one possibility among many, that the individual makes himself objective and contributes to the making of history. His project becomes a reality of which the agent is perhaps ignorant, but which, by means of the conflicts which history manifests and engenders, influences the course of events.' In every actual social situation one may describe both the objective facts—for instance, that there is at a given time a shortage of medical students—and the choices which therefore, because of these facts, are open to an individual man about to embark on a career. There are possibilities between which he chooses. And his circumstances are defined by the range of possibilities and the number of things which are ruled out for him.

The task which Sartre sets himself is the mapping out of human activity, viewed both from within and from without; and this will entail an analysis of the kinds of social group with which, as we have seen, a man is necessarily acquainted as soon as he is aware of the world at all; for it is within these social groups that his choices will be made. Praxis then appears as the instrument of the historical process, and it must be investigated for this reason; and it is also supposed to be the living proof that the dialectical process actually occurs. The particular role which existentialism has in the interpretation of the historical process is to insist upon the specificity of each historical event. It can also explain how a certain individual freely chooses his own nature from among the various possibilities open to him. This is illustrated in the *Question of Method* by a long analysis of the life of Flaubert.

Sartre's conclusion sums up the programme sketched out in the *Question of Method*. 'The dialectic', he says, 'can be seen as history and historical reason only through an examination of human praxis; which is itself unintelligible without the concepts of need, project, and "transcendence".' (This last is the going beyond the given situation to make actual changes in the world, which we have already noticed.) These, then, are the fundamental ideas of the programme. It is with the use of these tools that he proposes the grafting of existentialism upon Marxism, and at the same time the foundation of dialectical reason, in such a way as to make a science of man, or anthropology, possible.

It is clear at this stage in what way Sartre thinks that existentialism, which amounts to an insistence on man's capacity for free choice according to his own view of his situation, can improve Marxist theory, which claims to be a science. He says: 'It is not in doubt that Marxism appears today as the only possible anthropology which could be at the same time historical and structural [i.e. forming a systematic basis for explanation and prediction]. It is the only theory, too, which takes man in his totality, taking as a starting point, that is to say, the materiality of his condition. No other theory could offer another starting point, for this would be to offer a different man as the object of study. It is at the centre of the movement of Marxist thought that we detect a fault, in so far as, in spite of himself, the Marxist tends to eliminate the questioner, and make of the thing questioned the object of an absolute science. The very ideas which Marxist research uses to describe our historical society—exploitation, alienation, fetishization, reification, and so on—are the very ideas which lead back immediately to existentialist theory. Even the notion of praxis and that of dialectic, which are inseparably bound up with one another, are in contradiction with the intellectualist concept of an absolute science.'

We are back, then, at the starting point. Marxism is criticized for being unduly *a priori* and unduly dogmatic. Existentialism is going to remedy both these faults by its insistence upon the notion of free individual men. 'Marxism will become an inhuman anthropology if it does not embody in itself man as its very foundation.' And again: 'The foundation of anthropology is man himself, not as the object of practical science, but as a practical organism, producing science as a part of his praxis.' Finally, 'From the day when Marxist research takes on a human dimension (which is the existentialist project) as the foundation of its science of anthropology, existentialism itself will no longer have a *raison d'être*: absorbed, surpassed, and preserved by the totalizing movement of philosophy, it will cease to be a particular inquiry, in order to become the foundation of all inquiries.'

This, then, was Sartre's plan. But we have so far none but the most general terms in which to consider it. It may therefore be appropriate before going further to raise the question upon what Marxist doctrines *precisely* Sartre proposed to graft existentialism. What exactly did he think was the connexion between his view of man's place in the universe and that of Marx? Is there any more reason for his adopting Marxism than simply that he supposed it was the dominant philosophy? The answer to these questions is not straightforward. For one thing, Sartre's opinions have undergone a good deal of change. For another thing, there is necessarily a certain amount of doubt about how he interpreted those Marxist doctrines which he wished to adopt.

(5) Sartre's view of dialectical materialism in 1946

To take the first point—the change in Sartre's own position. It may be as well to look back at this stage to an essay published in 1946 in *Les Temps Modernes*, in which Sartre made his position at that time clear—not, it is true, with regard to Marx himself, but with regard to contemporary Marxist thought. It may then be easier to see what aspects of Marxist theory he thought could be improved by the addition of existentialism, and how his own ideas had to be modified in order to make this amalgamation possible.

In the essay, which has been translated under the title *Materialism and Revolution*, Sartre objects to the practice of offering to young men a supposedly clear and definite choice between Hegelian idealism on the one hand and materialism on the other. People, he says, are educated to think that Hegelian idealism is too optimistic, and yet at the same time hopeless, because too subjective, and therefore too little scientific. They are also taught that, if they reject this, the only alternative is materialism, and dialectical materialism at that. Sartre then criticizes the basic concepts of dialectical materialism.

In the first place, he somewhat confusedly tries to show that the notion of dialectical *materialism* is contradictory. For the essence of the dialectic is, he says, totality. (That this is so turns out, as we shall see later, to be a stumbling block for Sartre himself in the end.) 'In it [dialectic] phenomena are never isolated appearances. When they occur together, it is always within the high unity of a whole, and they are bound together by inner relationships; that is, the presence of one modifies the other in its inner nature.' But the universe of science with which materialism is exclusively concerned is quantitative; and 'the elements which compose it maintain only relationships of contiguity and simultaneity'. A quantitative element or unit is not affected by the presence of another unit; therefore the notion of

151

totalization, that is, of internal relations, must be absent from science; and therefore there can be no scientific or materialist dialectic.

The weak steps in this argument are very obvious. There is no examination of the view that 'material' means the same as 'scientific', a view which would be disputed by anyone who had read Marx. For Sartre is using 'scientific' here to mean 'quantitative', or at least 'translatable into quantitative terms'; while Marx means by 'materialism' something quite different, namely the insistence upon man's physical environment, rather than his thought, as the subject-matter of history. Moreover, Sartre's readiness to accept the intelligibility of dialectic in the Hegelian sense might be criticized. But in any case, having satisfied himself that no literal sense can be made of *dialectical* materialism, he goes on to suggest that materialism itself is not a rational set of beliefs but rather a *human attitude*.

No contemporary Marxist, Sartre says, is prepared to say why he accepts the materialist's account of nature and of history. He just accepts it. It is a matter of faith. So he concludes that the materialist faith is accepted as a useful myth. 'Materialism is indisputably the only myth that suits revolutionary requirements.' But he argues that a philosophy must be more than a myth; it must be true. It is the philosopher's task to elicit what truth there may be in materialism, and to construct it into a system as acceptable to the revolutionary as the myth was, but with the additional merit of being true.

The first step towards the construction of such a philosophy must be an analysis of the revolutionary mind. The revolutionary is, he says, both an oppressed person and a key-stone of the society which oppresses him. He is, that is to say, a member of the class which works for the dominant class. 'This double character of producer and oppressed person is sufficient to define the revolutionary's situation, but not the revolutionary himself.' For the revolutionary is a man who necessarily goes beyond the situation in which he finds himself. He wants to change his situation; and therefore he considers it from an historical point of view, with himself as an historical agent. We are reminded here of the analysis, in *Being and Nothingness*, of the motives behind revolution. Furthermore, being a worker, he sees human relationships from the point of view of work.

Work itself has a double sense; it is a direct link between men and the world of things, and it is also a primary relation between men and one another. The revolutionary's philosophy, then, is 'embodied in the original plan of the worker who joins the revolutionary party, and is implicit in his revolutionary attitude; for any plan for changing the world is inseparable from a certain understanding which reveals the world from the viewpoint of the change one wishes to bring about in it'. Revolutionary thinking is thus thinking within a given situation; and *action* to change the world must have primacy in a revolutionary system, rather than mere *knowledge* of the world as it is. 'What is needed, in a word, is a philosophical theory which shows that human reality is action, and that action upon the universe is identical with the understanding of that universe as it is, or, in other words, that action is the unmasking of reality, and, at the same time, a modification of that reality.' And to this Sartre adds a footnote: 'This is what Marx in his *Thesis on Feuerbach* calls "practical materialism". But why "materialism"?' Sartre is right to object to the word 'materialism' if this means, as he supposes, that everything said about the world should be expressible in terms of quantity. This is the dogma of which he, at this time, accuses Marxist theory. On the other hand, it is easy to see why he accepts the Marxist insistence on the practical. For it was at the very heart of the doctrines of *Being and Nothingness* that there is no such thing as bare perception of the world without action upon it, and that it is impossible to separate action from perception of the world as seen from a certain point of view, and as having certain features to be changed.

A few pages further on Sartre lays down a programme which a revolutionary philosophy ought to fulfil. It should show (i) that man is 'unjustifiable'—that his existence is contingent, in that neither he nor any Providence has produced it; (ii) that as a result of this, any collective order established by men can be replaced in the course of time, by other orders; (iii) that the system of values current in any society reflects the structure of that society and tends to preserve it; and (iv) that it can thus always be replaced by other systems which are not yet clearly perceived.

The possibility of men rising above a situation in order to achieve a general view of it, which is what the revolutionary philosopher would do, is what is meant by human freedom. No materialism, Sartre says, can explain this freedom. No system of causes and effects can 'make me look back at my situation in order to grasp it in its totality'. So materialism cannot account for class *consciousness*, without which revolution would be impossible.

Idealism, Sartre claims, deceives the revolutionary by teaching him that there is a set of duties and of values inherent in the order of things, given in the universe (the 'spirit of seriousness' is here taken to be characteristic of idealism). But materialism also deceives him, by robbing him of his freedom in a different way—by making him a part of inert nature, with no ability to transcend his situation. By adopting materialism—that is, determinism—the revolutionary is like Samson, 'who accepted burial in the ruins of the temple, provided that the Philistines perished with him'. For the slave is doing away with his own and his masters' freedom at one and the same time, by submerging both himself and them in *matter*. The revolutionary philosophy must be one which recognizes the freedom of man within his situation to assess this situation and change it. For this is the freedom which, as a matter of *fact*, man possesses.

'It is not true, then, that man is outside nature and the world, as the idealist has it, nor that he is only up to his ankles in it, like a bather shivering on the edge of the sea while his head is in the clouds. He is completely in nature's clutches, and at any moment nature can crush him and annihilate him, body and soul. He is in her clutches from the very beginning: for him, being born really means "coming into the world" in a situation not of his choice, with *this particular body*, *this* family and *this* race perhaps. But if he happens to plan, as Marx expressly states, to change the world, this means that he is, to begin with, a being for whom *the world* exists in its totality. . . . It is in changing the world that we come to know it. Neither the detached consciousness that would soar above the universe without being able to get a foothold on it, nor the material object which reflects a condition without understanding it, can ever "grasp" the totality of existence in a synthesis, even a purely conceptual one. Only a man, situated in the universe and *completely* crushed by the forces of nature and transcending them *completely* through his design to master them, can do this. It is the elucidation of the new ideas of "situation" and "being in the world" that revolutionary behaviour specifically calls for.'

This, then, was the new political philosophy which Sartre thought was needed and which he thought could be written in 1946. I have spent some time on his arguments against Marxism at that date, not only to get clear the historical development of his thought, but for its own sake. Though vague and rhetorical in parts, and at other times guilty of dressing up obvious truths to look like relevations, the essay which we have been considering is a powerful plea for a new political philosophy; and, more important, it shows what form this new philosophy might take. To one who had read, and been excited by reading, *Being and Nothingness*, and who then, after the war, read *Materialism and Revolution*, it must have seemed that Sartre really was going to restore the best in Marxist theory, by grafting on to it that analysis of man in his situation in the world, and of his freedom within his situation, which would be the existentialist contribution to political theory. Though Sartre made no such grandiose claim at this time, one might have been forgiven for thinking that a new political philosophy which was concrete and which truly fitted the facts was about to be born.

But in 1960—when, as we have seen, Sartre proposed to revivify Marxism—he also proposed to resurrect the materialist myth, on the strange grounds that it was the only possible philosophy to adopt at the present time. Even as late as 1957, when the *Question of Method* was first published, one might perhaps have hoped that some real alternative to the dichotomy between materialism and idealism was going to be offered: it would not have been absurd to hope that the proposal to 'interiorize' and render concrete the Marxist philosophy might result in a kind of political existentialism, in which individual freedom was still the starting point. But in 1960, with the publication of Volume I of *The Critique of Dialectical Reason*, we are obliged to admit that Marxism has taken over, and that existentialism is only an added trick, if so much—an 'ideology' at best, and therefore, in the long run, dispensable. Moreover, it is the fully grown Marx-Engels doctrine of dialectical materialism which has taken over— the very doctrine which, in 1946, Sartre claimed to find actually contradictory.

(6) The development of Marxist thought

At this point it is necessary to digress a little in order to distinguish between certain Marxist doctrines, roughly between the early and late theories of Marx. For, on the face of it, there is more in common between existentialism and the early theories of Marx, which dealt with alienated man, the individual within society, than between existentialism and the later theories of dialectical materialism and the class struggle. Yet it is to the later Marx that Sartre succumbs in the end. The explanation of this odd fact seems to lie in a parallel development in Marx and in Sartre; for it can, I think, be shown that the later doctrines of Marx do not constitute a complete break with the earlier but grow out of them intelligibly, becoming more and more general in their subject-matter under the influence of Feuerbach and Engels. And in the same way the Sartre of *Being and*

Nothingness seems to have developed into the Sartre of the *Critique* through abandoning, under the influence of Marx, the individual for the group, and psychology for sociology. Already in *Being and Nothingness*, as we have seen, the need to do this in order to produce an actual morality was foreshadowed.

There is, naturally, some difficulty and doubt in the interpretation of Marx, and this is not the place to enter into a detailed discussion of his development. But of the fact that his early writings show more affinity with existentialism than his later there can be no doubt. For in the early writings Marx was concerned with the revolution as a means of *individual salvation*. The revolution is worth supporting not for its material benefits, though it would bring these to some, nor, naturally, because it was going to happen anyway, but because by its means alone would men be freed from the bonds which, in the course of their history, they had forged for themselves in society. The most important element in a man's life is the work that he does. But in society as it is, this work itself is *alienated*; that is to say, a man does not work freely, and for himself, as a means of self-realization. He gets from his work only financial benefit, and little of that; but he is bound to it by what seem like ineluctable economic forces. He cannot *not* work; but work, for him personally, is futile.

Work, for Marx, is the essentially human activity. Only men are capable of intervening in the material world in precisely this way. Because men are uniquely capable of this deliberate acting upon and changing the world it is this kind of activity which has the highest potential value for each individual, and by means of it he will be saved from oppression, if he is to be saved. There is nothing else but human praxis which has value in itself. But in society as it is he suffers from alienation. Men who are free to change their condition nevertheless feel bound by it, and believe themselves to be under the power of *things*—of impersonal economic forces. If they realized their situation, they could change it. Alienation, then, in this individualistic theory, is surprisingly like Bad Faith, the false belief that one is bound to go on as one is, the denial of freedom.

(7) Alienation and the division of labour

Perhaps it is through the concept of 'alienation' that one can hope for most light on the development of Marx's thought, and so, indirectly, on the development of Sartre as well. For Hegel, alienation was an inevitable condition of man, as long as man distinguished between subject, himself, and object, the world. As we have seen, Hegel believed that there was only one world, the world of spirit or idea, and that therefore the distinction between myself and the outside world was delusory. Knowledge is the repossession within myself of what has been falsely divided from me; so an increase in knowledge is a lessening of the condition of alienation, in which the true self is divided and estranged from itself. The world is mine; but by treating it as an object, I conceal this from myself. This estrangement is what we aim to eliminate as we aim to know more and more. The external world is a hostile world, not because for each of us it is experienced as a personal hostility (in the way in which, in *Being and Nothingness*, we are supposed to experience the look of the Other) but because the concept of spirit *is* the concept of the whole world, and the division of the world into two parts is a negation of this totality and is therefore contradictory. The hostility is logical incompatibility, and is not felt as a passion. Alienation is necessary, and man necessarily strives to overcome it.

Now Marx, as a young man, accepted Hegelianism with the greatest enthusiasm; and what seems to have appealed to him particularly was the notion that there is only one world, and that therefore there can be no values outside humanity itself. Man exists as part of the world; he cannot aspire to move outside it; and anything to which he ascribes value must itself be a part of the very same concrete world. The vast difference between Hegelian idealism, in which possession of the world by knowledge was the aim, and

Marxist materialism, where, instead, men aimed to master the world by working upon it, may tend to obscure the essential similarity between them: both insisted that it was wrong to think of man as separate from the world. There are not two worlds but one, and when men think of themselves as separate from the world this is alienation.

So Marx also accepted the Hegelian concept of alienation, but with a difference. The one world which exists, for him, is the world of concrete reality, here and now, not the Hegelian fantasy-world of thought or spirit. Hegel's vision of self-alienated man was accepted by Marx, but self-realization—the overcoming of alienation—is not envisaged as primarily a matter of knowing more, of understanding, or of science, but rather of action. But man cannot realize himself unless the circumstances of his life are radically altered; for his circumstances, being hostile, are what cause him to become estranged from himself. Alienation, the belief that one is surrounded by forces disconnected from and inimical to oneself, is everywhere in man's life. It is an illusion indeed, but it can be removed only by altering the circumstance in which it grew up. Marx wrote, in the fourteenth thesis on Feuerbach: 'The demand to remove illusions about one's situation is a demand to renounce a situation that required illusions.'

In the political sphere alienation meant the domination of men by the concept of the state—an *object* separate from, and hostile to, themselves. The only cure for this was to get rid of the state. Later, Marx began to concentrate particularly on the notion of alienated *labour* and on economic alienation. Alienated labour was work performed by men in a state of self-estrangement so that, as we have seen already, a man feels bound to work, compelled to by the hostile force of economic necessity; but he does not feel that in working he is freely undertaking the kind of creative labour which fulfils himself, though in fact there is no other means but work by which he could fulfil his nature. Alienated man works only for money, under the pressure of egoistic need. Money is for him an inhuman force. To cure this alienation the conditions of labour have to be radically altered. Thus more and more clearly *revolution* emerges as the cure for man's alienated condition. And gradually Marx took on the idea of the proletariat (first mentioned in 1843, in the Introduction to Hegel's *Philosophy of Right*) as a substitute for the Hegelian concept of man. The proletariat first stood as a symbol for alienated man, and then actually became identified with alienated man, striving to overcome alienation by revolution. This was the essential form of Marxist theory up to 1844.

By the time that the *Communist Manifesto* was published by Marx and Engels in 1848, alienated man had disappeared altogether from the scene. The conflicts spoken of in this book are not conflicts between man and himself but between class and class. Marx had become convinced that man's self-estrangement could be understood only as a *social* relation, a relation of group to group. Thus what appeared first as a psychological theory about individuals turned gradually into a sociological theory about the relation of class to hostile class. It is *society* which is split in two now, not the individual; and Marx pours scorn on the idea of man as an object about whose essential nature one can say anything at all. Alienation is transformed into war—war between the workers and the capitalists; and finally the word itself drops out. Linked with the theory of the warring classes is the theory that history has developed, and could only have developed, through this war. And so the Hegelian dialectic, which at first consisted in a clash of contradictory ideas, becomes an actual war, the class war.

Moreover, even the fact, which Marx still acknowledges, that men feel themselves bound to work but do not properly benefit by it, is no longer explained by the hypothesis of the work's being done by man in a state of estrangement from himself. Instead he says that the sense of the hostility of the external world is to be explained by the fact that men work to produce this world within the system of the *division of labour*. It would be easy to regard this as a total break from the earlier theory of alienated labour. But it is possible to argue that even the notion of the division of labour is only the sociological expression of the old notion of individual self-alienation. In one of the manuscripts of 1844 Marx brought the two ideas together, though in a very obscure way; and from now on the division of labour is made responsible for all the ills for which alienation was blamed before. Even the state is hostile because of it. So, in the *Critique of the Gotha Programme*, Marx wrote: 'By the word "state" is meant the government machine, or the state in so far as it forms a special organism separated from society, through the division of labour.' Specialization is thus the root of the tyranny of the state; it is also that which, in general, makes it impossible for a man to realize himself individually, because it defeats his class.

To sum up, then, the class conflict is the expression of the hostility inherent in a system which permits the division of labour. 'Materialism' for Marx means the theory that it is men working on, and being worked on by, the material world which constitutes the whole of what there is. This materialism is essentially an historical theory because it contains the concept of *change* in the real world. Dialectical materialism is, then, the history of the conflict of one class with another, whenever the material suffering of one class has, due to the division of labour, become intolerable.

(8) Summary of the 'Critique of Dialectical Reason'

Coming then at last to the *Critique of Dialectical Reason* itself, we must try to see how the promised grafting of existentialism upon this final and mature Marxist dialectic actually goes. When one begins to read the *Critique* the promise that Marxism was to be made concrete and personal seems peculiarly empty. On the contrary, the abstractions of Marxist theory seem to have run riot, and to have been allowed to get entirely out of hand. New terms are introduced, new technicalities invented; and the concrete world of things, the world of real people, with which Sartre

F

had always presented us before, seems entirely to have vanished. The best that can be attempted first of all is a summary of the argument of the *Critique*, in so far as there is one, simplified as much as the ramifications of technical terms will allow. In this way it may be possible to judge what Sartre has made of Marxist theory, and what has happened to his own philosophy in the meantime.

The *Critique* opens with an introduction, formally similar to the introduction to Kant's *Critique of Pure Reason*, setting out the aims of the undertaking (namely to found Dialectical Reason *a priori*), with an account of the faults of dogmatism to be found in Marxism in its current form. Book I is divided into four sections, the first of which contains an account of the notion, which we have seen to be fundamental, of individual 'praxis', or free human intervention in the world. It is this concept which, properly understood, is the foundation of dialectical reasoning, the reasoning which proves itself to be necessary by its means.

Four questions are raised at the beginning of this section. First, how can praxis be at the same time an experience of necessity and of liberty? Second, how can dialectical reason both see history as a whole and at the same time take account of the acts of individuals? Thirdly, if dialectic is directed towards understanding the present in terms of the past and the future, how can it have a future of its own in history? And fourth, if dialectic is to be materialist, how are we to understand the peculiar materialism of human praxis and its connexion with materialism of other kinds? Of these, the third seems to be the most difficult to attach meaning to; but it may be taken together with the second as a demand for an explanation of the essentially historical and developing nature of Marxist thought. The first and the fourth are both directly concerned with the nature of praxis, as we actually experience it. And it is to this subject that Sartre immediately addresses himself.

(a) *Praxis—work in the context of scarcity*
Praxis, he says, is work; and work itself is the effort to

satisfy our needs by means of projects formed in our world, which is essentially a world of *scarcity*. Thus at the very beginning the two key concepts need (*besoin*) and scarcity (*rarité*) are introduced. The notion of praxis is necessarily connected with that of need. Although it is a contingent fact that we live among scarcity, yet if we did not, our idea of praxis would be different.

It is this definition which Sartre hopes to use in order to show that our undertaking work in the world of need proves, as we do it, that our reasoning about the world must be dialectical, progressing by the overcoming of contradictions. The proof is obscure, and seems to turn partly on the variety of senses of the word 'negation' which Sartre is able to deploy. He appears to regard the negation of a proposition as identical with the contradicting of that proposition, and thus he speaks either of 'negation' or 'contradiction' indifferently. The proof seems to come to something like this: from the fact that we experience the world as a series of needs, it follows that we experience it negatively, as consisting of things we have not got and fields we have not conquered. Work is essentially the changing of the material world to overcome these negations. We regard the material world as a place in which we may fulfil our ends; and each end fulfilled is a completion. So we necessarily aim at completions. We conceive tasks before us by conceiving an end which is the overcoming of an obstacle, itself something we realize negatively. 'Work could not exist . . . except as totalization, and as the overcoming of contradictions.'

So far, Sartre admits, nothing much has been said about reality, since man working in isolation (from which the definition derives) is a mere abstraction, of which an example could never be found in the world; but what he hopes to have done is to show that for each man, through his most ordinary everyday experience, which is that of work, the necessity of the dialectic proves itself all the time. The dialectical character of action, the overcoming of negations by intervention in the material world, is, he thinks, self-evident. By the end of this section Sartre has provided material out of which the answers to his four questions could be devised, though they are never directly answered.

(b) *The nature of materialism*

The second section deals perhaps more directly with the fourth question: in what sense are we to understand materialism in the context of human action? This must be the most important question of all for a materialist; for it goes without saying that it is upon the inadequacy of materialism to account for apparently free human action that critics, including Sartre himself at an earlier stage, always concentrate. But he does not here appear to attach much importance to the difficulty. We are face to face with the paradox that the materialism which he decried in 1946 is just accepted, lock, stock, and barrel, in 1960, without many questions asked. He regards the relation between one human being and another as occupying a kind of mean position between purely material relations on the one hand, and relations of thought which are the product of material relations on the other. He introduces the topic of human relations in a pleasingly concrete way, though the concreteness is short-lived. He imagines himself sitting at the window of an hotel, doing nothing himself, but observing two workmen, one each side of a brick wall; he can see them both from above, but they are unaware of one another. He can describe them both as 'men working'. But he has to describe them *separately*. To think of them both as aiming at the same things, employed in the same activity, would be to falsify the situation.

From this simple scene he draws a specifically anti-Kantian moral. There is no such thing as a kingdom of ends; and it is wrong to speak of treating *humanity* as an end. Nothing can be an end for itself except an idea, he says. For any concrete human being must, being partly a material thing, be capable of being used as a means, or a tool; and by working he must choose to use himself as a tool, and so as a means to something *else*. Thus only idealism, which is already discredited, could subscribe to the Kantian view that humanity constitutes an absolute end. For an end is a concept, something envisaged; and humanity is concrete, not a mere idea. We must recognize that, as with the workmen on either side of the wall, each man has his own end; and what he aims at is to change his status as a man. So far from treating himself and others as ends in themselves, each man treats himself as an instrument of change, as a means of becoming what he is not. Kant believed in a static, permanent, single end—humanity. Sartre (and Marx) substitute a changing and developing end. There could be no change unless each one envisaged for himself a situation which is not yet realized.

So far, then, we have learned only that human praxis is directed to a goal which is beyond the present time; but we have been told nothing of what that goal is (except that it is not 'humanity itself'), nor why it is that men wish to change their status. Nor have we learned anything at all about praxis as the revelation of dialectical *necessity*.

This topic is, however, introduced in the third section, albeit somewhat confusedly. Materiality, or the fact that the world is entirely material, shows itself in the human environment in a particular form, namely in the form of scarcity. 'The whole human adventure is a struggle against scarcity.' Scarcity is the moving force of history. Although it is a contingent fact that scarcity exists (one could imagine a universe without it), nevertheless it is the fundamental human relation, as things are, relating men both to nature or material objects, and to one another. It is scarcity which makes us exactly what we are, with just the history we have. It is scarcity, and the determination to overcome it, which motivates individual human praxis; but it is also scarcity which lies behind the general movement of history. Because of scarcity, men are the opponents of one another. I regard everyone else as a threat to myself, and I am aware that I am a threat to others. 'Each feels in each other the principle of evil' (p. 221). So it is in this way, as a threat, that other people feature in the environment in which I exercise my power to change things. So far from regarding others as ends in themselves, I regard them as obstacles to my ends.

It is perhaps worth remarking upon the obvious contrast between the hostility which exists between human beings here and in the world of *Being and Nothingness*. There, the Other was my enemy, and he existed as a threat to me, but this was for inescapable psychological reasons. We were enemies because we had incompatible designs upon one another, which arose of necessity out of our feelings and our desires. Here, we are contingently at war, because of a feature of our environment. We need not necessarily war for ever. It is possible that Sartre thinks that he is accounting for the same perceptible facts in two different ways. But it is more probable that he now thinks that the fact of human hostility *is* contingent, and can be overcome like other features of our environment. But he never himself mentions the earlier doctrines, here or elsewhere in the book.

There is another sense, too, in which men do not treat each other, or indeed themselves, as ends: by their work they partly reduce themselves to the status of material things, in order to be able to act on other material things, to change their environment. That is, men literally become *tools* for changing things. And this is how what starts as a mere thought or project comes to have the physical power to effect changes on the physical world. Praxis gives us experience both of human beings and of the material world. But if men could not become tool-like in making changes in their environment they could do nothing; there would be no such thing as praxis. If, for example, I want to pump up my bicycle it is no use merely understanding the mechanism of a bicycle pump. Even if I had invented the pump myself it would not help me to blow up the tyres unless I could use it. And using it involves using myself, my own fingers and muscles, as part of the operation of fitting the pump to the wheel, and moving its parts. Pure cerebration will not get anything done. The physical aspect of the human being is, quite literally, his contact with the world; and by using himself, his own limbs, as instruments, he changes things. Tools are merely extensions of our hands; or we may think of both hands and pump as tools.

All this is, as it were, the raw material out of which we can construct an account of our experience of necessity. The experience of necessity itself is next introduced (p. 279). But when we come to the point, Sartre has extraordinarily little more to say about it. Necessity, he tells us, is not to be confused with restraint. In our activity we experience freedom, in that we plan what to do; the decisions are our own, and freely made. But we also experience necessity, in the fact of the otherness of other people and of the physical world, and in the fact that often what we plan turns out differently from what we had envisaged, and yet we recognize it as our own work. 'The man who looks at his work and recognizes himself there entirely, and yet at the same time does not recognize himself there at all; who can say at one and the same time "I did not want that" and "I understand that this is what I have made, and I could not have done anything else"—it is this man who grasps necessity in an immediate dialectical movement, as the inevitable fate of freedom when it comes into contact with the external world.'

So praxis is said to show us necessity, and dialectical necessity at that. For a man who freely starts by working upon matter is, by the dialectical next step, worked upon by the very matter which he has worked to produce. He starts by making objects, and the objects end by making him. They determine what he can do, and define his peculiar facticity. Here, then, is Sartre's version of Marxist alienation; and by means of it men become parts of the material environment. Sartre wishes to assert not only that this happens but that our way of getting to know that it happens, by actually experiencing it, has a special kind of status: knowledge gained in this way is incontrovertible, since to deny it would be to deny that one is doing what one is doing.

(c) *The collective*
So far, we have been shown the human situation as it is

given in individual projects, or in the experience of the individual in his working life. But this is a mere abstraction. In the fourth section Sartre introduces us to the social structure which reflects the basic facts of scarcity and man-as-dangerous-to-man, namely the *collective*. Being made a part of the material environment in order to change it, which in the third section was said to be the effect of the dialectic of praxis, is equivalent to what Sartre calls 'atomization'. When men are atomized, they have become like tools lying side by side in a box—all to be of use in changing the world but unable to initiate anything. 'Atomization' is the name given to the human condition of separateness of one man from another, and this plurality is manifested in the collective.

The essential characteristic of a collective, as opposed to a *group*, is that in it men live side by side without any sense of community. They are still a number of individuals; and the law of their co-existence is that of a *series*. Sartre gives us a small-scale example of such a collective in the case of a bus-queue. A bus-queue is nothing but a 'plurality of solitudes'. There is, in a sense, a common end, to get on to the bus when it comes. But the community of the end is delusory; for each member of the queue wants to catch the bus for his own separate reason; he does not care whether the others catch the bus or not, and if there is too little room on the bus he prefers that he should catch it rather than that they should. But they form themselves into a queue rather than standing in no order at all, to settle who shall get on the bus first, since it is clear that there is no intrinsic characteristic of any of them which is such as to determine who ought to get on first. Therefore they settle the matter in this purely numerical way; no matter what his qualities or his deserts, the man at the front of the queue is number one, and he gets on first.

This impossibility of deciding who is *de trop* on the basis of intrinsic qualities amounts to the acceptance by each member of the collective of his role as what Sartre calls a *general individual*, an individual with no specific characteristics. If there are more individuals of this sort than one, then each is interchangeable with any other. If all social life were lived at the level of the collective there would be no institutions, no leaders, and no organization for the sake of efficiency. Everyone would be as powerless as everyone else. As a member of this mere series none has any power to overcome the fact that, as material bodies, all the members are separate. The revelation to each of this impotence is, according to Sartre, the most important moment in the change from collective to group—in the history, that is to say, of the movement towards the revolution. 'The series becomes apparent to each one . . . at the moment when he grasps in his own person and that of others their joint powerlessness to overcome their material differences' (p. 325).

The identification of myself with all others, or rather with any other at all, is next illustrated by means of an economic example, that of the stock market in a capitalist society, where the behaviour of each buyer and seller is always determined by what is going on elsewhere. Everyone has a self-interested motive which, artificially, takes into account the self-interest of others. The motive of *my* buying or selling is the consideration of what other buyers and sellers are doing. But we are each out for ourselves alone. This is 'seriality'. According to Sartre, serial existence such as this explains a whole range of social phenomena; for, though we do not live entirely at the level of seriality, yet this is our condition in large areas of our everyday life. Such phenomena as panic, colonialism, mere crazes of one sort or another, are explained by seriality, where public opinion determines our opinions, and there is no motive for saying, for instance, that a certain popular record is the best except that everyone says so. That is to say, a record is best because it sells most, and it sells most because it is the 'pick of the pops'—the best. The serial state is the negation of the dialectic, in that it is the negation of progress and freedom.

The next dialectical movement comes into being with the origin of 'the group', which is constructed precisely to destroy the collective and the inhuman conditions imposed by the serial relation between men. The discussion of the formation of the group occupies Book II of the *Critique*.

(d) *The formation of the group*

Book II is entitled *Du Groupe à L'Histoire*. The bulk of it is taken up with examples designed to illustrate the emergence of the group from the collective. This emergence falls into two stages: the group in fusion, and the group proper. It would be impossible fully to do justice to the book without analysing the historical examples in detail, but this task must be left to an historian. All that can be done by one who is interested primarily in philosophy is to try to extract from the details certain general theses which are insisted upon in the course of the examples, and to infer from these what philosophical conclusions Sartre might be willing to draw from them. But it must be emphasized that the extraction from this part of the book of anything like a philosophical doctrine *is* a matter of inference, and indeed of interpretation. It is perfectly possible that one may get it wrong.

The description of man's lapse into seriality on contact with the physical world, which occupies Book I of the *Critique*, has been described as Sartre's version of the Fall. The rise of 'the group' is his battle against this fallen state. The best example of this struggle is drawn from the history of the French Revolution. Sartre analyses the 14th of July 1789 in order to show how, at a moment of crisis and under threat from a manifestly hostile group, the Parisians, who had till then been wandering isolated from one another in a maze of separate roads and alleys, came to realize the unity of one part of Paris. The sense of unity in the teeth of opposition grew, until finally there came into being a genuine self-conscious community of ends, a real reciprocity. Each man, in the face of common danger, identified himself with his neighbour, so that other people ceased to determine a man's conduct from the outside but came instead to determine it from within, in the way in which a man determines his own conduct. Instead of regarding other people as obstacles, I may come to identify them, in this sort of situation, with my own will. What I plan is, literally, what they plan, and their will and mine are one.

The critical moment, then, in the struggle to form a group is the moment when I regard others as, each of them, my *alter ego*. The movement out of the collective towards the group is dialectical. Sartre is concerned to show that one can deduce the necessity of *this* dialectical movement from the necessity which, in Book I, he hoped to have shown we experience directly in our individual acts. That is to say, he does not treat the collective, or the group, as an organic entity with a life and a dynamic force of its own: it has not got its own laws of development; it is governed by the laws of the development of the individual. The group is 'the communal structure of *my act*' (p. 403). Its reality is the reality of the 'general individual', but this individual is no longer a separate isolated atomic thing, whose only relation to other individuals is the antagonism created by need. Each, in the group, has found himself in other people— so that, as we have seen, other people are now the source of his liberty, not the obstacles to it. Revolutionary power, then, is not to be found in the rising class, but in the dynamic group of individuals, which becomes a force in history as they, the individuals, emerge from the state of the collective. The moment of the emergence of what may be called the 'general will', when men truly identify themselves with one another, is perhaps the moment when the hopelessness of man's situation as an individual is overcome. If this moment could be prolonged, men would co-operate instead of fighting, and the ethics promised in *Being and Nothingness* would be complete.

But the problem which faces the group, since it has neither organic nor natural unity, is always how to remain in existence, how to avoid lapsing back into the impotence of the mere collective. The risk of the group's dissolving is acute at the moment when the immediate danger which brought it into being passes. The chief means of avoiding dissolution is the *oath*, which imposes an artificial necessity upon everyone, in place of the new-found liberty of the group; and the sanction of the oath, without which it would have no power, is terror. In the oath I recognize the right of everyone else over me—their right to kill me if I default. What has been formed by such an oath is a real community, bound with a 'fraternity of fear'. We are not bound to any fraternity by a common nature, any more than peas in a pod are a fraternity; but we are bound by the deliberate act of recognition of the right of each over the others. Sartre says of the formation of the group, that, so far from being *founded on* our common humanity, it itself is 'the beginning of humanity'.

(e) *The organization of the group*

Most of the rest of the book is taken up with examples designed to show how the group, once formed, becomes an organization with institutions, laws, and special tasks allotted to individuals. If what is now being discussed is a state or political group, then the question naturally arises of where the sovereignty in this state resides. To this Sartre answers that, while in the collective the concept of sovereignty has no place, since everyone is as powerless as everyone else, in the group the opposite is true—everyone is sovereign. The problem of sovereignty in the ordinary sense is a problem of the limitation of a sovereignty that is universal. The conclusion of this part is that the historical development of all societies is a function of the fundamental contradiction between the inert inhuman series and the fraternity of the group; it is this contradiction which is the moving force of history. But one cannot describe either the serial collective or the group except in terms of individuals and the relations which they bear towards other individuals.

(9) Totalization

I have devoted more space to the analysis of the first part of the *Critique* than of the second, since it is in the first that we find the general tools with which Sartre proposes to bring about his reform of Marxist theory. Moreover, the second volume of the whole book, if it is ever written, will continue the subject-matter of the second part, although from the point of view of 'reflexive experience'; so there is some case for saying that one's judgment of the second part should be reserved for the present. But if we are to look anywhere for what is generally accounted political theory, it is in this second part of Volume I that we should expect to find it.

In the first part we learn with what concepts Sartre intends to analyse societies; in the second he at least embarks on the analysis. But the upshot seems to me disappointing in more ways than one. There is a haunting sense, which increases as one reads these densely packed, rebarbative pages, that this has been said before in a very different style. The passage in which 'the oath' is introduced as the bond which holds society together, which is born of terror and kept in life by terror, finally convinces one that this is the voice of Hobbes. It is not, I think, unduly fanciful to see the dreaded state of seriality as the counterpart of the war of all against all in the state of nature; to see the oath backed up by terror as the covenant supported by the sword. And both Hobbes and Sartre are concerned somehow to explain how, being material objects composed of material atoms, men get into the condition of setting up institutions and establishing laws. There are, of course, vast differences. But both in Hobbes and in Sartre we are at a loss to know whether the reconstruction of the growth of institutions is entirely *a priori*, or partly empirical.

Sartre claims to be practising anthropology; and his examples are all historical, and drawn from recent history. Moreover, he claims that it is only contingently, not necessarily, true that scarcity is the normal condition of man. But suppose that there were no historical examples to be found of the passage from the series to the group; suppose, that is, that he were not lucky enough to have the French Revolution to draw upon; would he have to give up the theory? It may be objected that this is a foolish question, since he might be thought to have used the theory just in order to explain the facts of the Revolution. But I do not think that this would be very plausible. Dialectical materialism is primarily an *a priori* system; and Sartre's version of it, in which the dynamic force within the dialectic process is individual human action—this is also *a priori*, though supposed to be capable of conclusive proof through the experience of each of us. So *if* historical examples should fail, the system would remain intact. But, of course, they need never fail, for anything whatever can be so described that it fits into the scheme of the human struggle to avoid the lapse into the impotence of seriality. Sartre accused the Marxists of forcing history into their pre-ordained pattern. Perhaps inevitably, he falls into the very same trap himself.

There is one further and important feature which is common to both Hobbes and Sartre, though to many other political theorists as well, and that is their insistence that the result of the contract or oath is *one unified society* which can be thought of as a whole, in terms of its common purpose. Sartre, it is true, in this volume of the *Critique*, is primarily interested in the supposed dialectical process towards the emergence of this unified society; but the dialectical process necessarily gives rise to something which can be completely grasped as one. The concept of the totality, though it is never clearly formulated, dominates the second half of Volume I of the *Critique*. In the first part the same concept was implied, but less clearly. For there the individual's work, his intervention in the physical world with the motive of satisfying some need, brought about in the physical world a change which could be fully described, as a whole, in terms of the intention of the individual; that is, the dialectic there came into being through some individual's forming a project the description of which involved viewing the situation as a whole, and rising above it. But in the second part, in which the acts of all the individuals are thought of as concerted, not only is the upshot of their acting a changed situation which can be totally described in terms of their (now) joint aim, but also the situation is created in which there is a kind of *identity* between one person and another; and the 'totalized' result is a *group* with one purpose in one complete organization.

This totalization, the goal of dialectic, inevitably strikes us as sinister in this context; and the identification of one individual with another seems to us to amount to the suppression of individual liberty, in the pursuit of some common human end. The 'fraternity of fear' pleases us as little as the absolute monarchy which, in Hobbes, produced the unity of the state. And Sartre freely admits that totalitarianism is part of the spirit of the age. In an essay published in *Situations II* he said: 'The totalitarian idea is part of the spirit of the age; it is that which inspired the Nazi experiment, the Marxist experiment and now the Existentialist experiment.'

But still, though all the examples in Part II are more strictly political than historical, and though serialism is clearly to be identified with capitalism, and communism with the true group, this is no more than one would expect. There is no point in contrasting, in general, the sort of situation which Sartre seems to regard as desirable with some vaguely liberal situation which we may feel we should prefer. Both the incompleteness of the book and its avowedly abstract and theoretical purpose make this kind of comment inappropriate. But what we have a right to demand is that the notion of 'the totality', fundamental to the last part of Volume I, should actually make sense— that is, that the adoption of the doctrine of 'totalization' should not be in contradiction with that grafting of existentialism upon Marxism which is the avowed purpose of the whole undertaking. And this demand cannot, I think, be satisfied.

In *Being and Nothingness* Sartre said: 'It is in principle impossible to adopt "the point-of-view of all".' And it is surely true that existentialism, if it is to retain any sort of identity at all, must essentially adopt the point-of-view of the individual. It must attempt to describe the world from behind the eyes of each man, uncommitted as far as possible by *a priori* theory. And even if existentialism were not theoretically committed to such an enterprise, in Sartre's hands at least its greatest successes have lain in the field of description. It is true that we are told, in the *Critique*, that the group is not an organic unity, that its existence is the existence of the individuals which compose it, viewed in a certain light. We are told, further, that the concept of the group-in-fusion cannot be intelligibly described except in terms of the individual effect on the outside world of individual praxis, and that the *a priori* foundation of Marxist theory is to be found in this individual praxis. But, unfortunately, merely saying that two things are compatible does not make them so; and there remains a fundamental and unbridgeable gap between the goal of the dialectical development of the group, and the world of individual projects to which we were introduced in *Being and Nothingness*.

Another way of regarding this same gap would be to concentrate on the difference between the personal apprehension of the world which each one of us has, and any systematic and objective science. Sartre criticized Marxists in the 1946 essay for thinking that the scientific and material was identical with the quantitative. He has abandoned that belief, if it was ever held, and instead he claims to prove the necessity of dialectical materialism from the starting point of individual apprehension. Dialectical necessity is, obviously, systematic; it is a rationalization of everything within one huge scientific scheme. Sartre seems to hope that he has effected a transition from an irrational and personal view of the world to the systematic and complete account of it. But the whole bulk of the *Critique* so far does not seem to me in the least to have narrowed the gap between the two. The upshot is only that Marxism can be seen to have swallowed up existentialism.

(10) The disappearance of the individual

One can perhaps understand to some extent the way this
has happened. There was, as we have seen, in the writings
of Marx a gradual change of interest from the individual
and his alienation from himself, to the group or class at
war with other classes because of the division of labour.
There is a closely parallel movement in Sartre's interests,
away from the point-of-view of the individual to the point-
of-view of all. But while there was nothing in Marx's
theory to prevent such a change, in Sartre's case it produces
a hopeless tension, since the theory from which he started
was precisely designed to show the impossibility of such an
'objective' position as that to which he has moved. Moreover, the change was not what he himself led us to expect
when he promised to 'interiorize' and make concrete the
theories of Marx. What we were entitled to expect was that
such Marxist concepts as 'alienation', 'division of labour',
and so on should be explained and examined from the
point-of-view of the person who is living through them;
we might expect to be told what these phenomena are
actually like—to be given their '*verité vécue*'. But instead
Sartre introduces a new set of concepts, no less abstract
than Marx's own, which, though they have in nearly every
case their analogues in the psychological concepts of *Being
and Nothingness*, are not really explained by these nor
shown to grow out of them. They just take over. For
example, as we have noticed earlier in this chapter, in
Being and Nothingness there existed between any two
conscious beings a state of conflict which, in the extreme
case of lovers, became a hopeless struggle by each to
possess the other completely, while leaving him free so
that he could freely give his love. This conflict in the
Critique has been watered down, and is now nothing but
an antagonism caused by the contingent phenomenon of
scarcity. It is the motive force of history, but it does not
seem to be in any way connected with facts about what

people are like—or only with the crudest facts, such as that they want enough to eat.

Again, there is a parallel, though a less close one, between the status of the individual consciousness which is frozen by the look of the Other, paralysed by the attributes which the Other applies to it and thus deprived of freedom, and the status in the *Critique* of the individual members of a collective who, merely by the circumstance of living in a community with others, are rendered impotent by the law of seriality. Their powerlessness is, first and foremost, a matter of circumstance; and this is illustrated by the example of the bus-queue. When the circumstances are altered, as they can be, the condition is mitigated or cured. Once again, the familiar concepts are changed and rendered 'scientific', with the result that a solution to difficulties is offered by means of revolutions. Whereas, in *Being and Nothingness*, there is no escape from the threat constituted by other people, in the *Critique* the threat can be averted by the formation and preservation of the group. Over and over again we can see this change. The 'project' of *Being and Nothingness*, which is the exercise of free choice, becomes 'praxis' in the *Critique*, in which is discovered dialectical rationality. The existentialist metaphysical philosophy itself becomes a dispensable ideology.

But these changes are not just whimsical; nor do they arise simply out of a snap conversion to Marxism. We saw at the end of the last chapter that some such move was made necessary by the impasse of *Being and Nothingness* itself. For not only there, but in the plays and novels of that period as well, a certain gloomy view of the human position was given us, and we were offered no way in which it was even logically possible to make things better. Since our condition was presented as part of the inevitable structure of the world, to ask what we ought to do to remedy it was futile. But now a course is presented to us as preferable to any other, namely to promote revolution; and this is something which we can do. When Sartre promised to write from an ethical standpoint this turned out to be impossible without a radical conversion. The only acceptable conversion, he has discovered, is a conversion to Marxism; for only this can make possible what had come to seem impossible at the end of *Being and Nothingness*, namely the growth of any relation between one person and another in society. The ethical problem must be the problem of how to treat others, and how to take their interests into account, to treat them as something other than a threat. The conversion is supposed to have shown the way to treating the interests of others as identical with one's own, and to regarding other people as brothers. It is the end of isolation.

But still this newly possible ethical theory does not satisfy us, nor should it wholly satisfy Sartre. At the end of *Being and Nothingness*, and by implication in the 1946 essay, the moral standpoint most severely criticized was that of *seriousness*. The 'spirit of seriousness', or idealism, led people to think that there were absolute values inherent in things and discoverable by men. In the political context it was this spirit which led the bourgeoisie to suppose themselves in some way naturally privileged, and, though not fully aware of themselves as a class, nevertheless to display solidarity in the belief that it was *naturally right* for things to go on as they were. In place of this Sartre wanted, in 1946, to put a philosophy which would conclusively demonstrate to each human being his own contingency. No one has any natural *raison d'être*, nor any natural right over anyone else. In the new morality, seriality, in which everyone is as *de trop* as everyone else and comes to feel that he is, is replaced by 'the group'; and this looks like a move away from contingency. But even in the group there are no natural rights. The fusion, the change from the collective to the group, is brought about by people who happen to want to change their circumstances, and who come to see themselves as bound by this common purpose. But so far from thereafter thinking of some members as privileged, they cannot exist as a group if they cease to think of themselves as in some way collectively identical. Institutions and authority have no natural existence. They come into being only by the artificial means of 'the oath'. The contingency of values is preserved by the contingency of institutions, which are deliberately chosen and can always be changed. So 'seriousness' is avoided, while at the same time a means of breaking down isolation has been found.

Nevertheless, in a different way, the characteristic existentialist contingency *has* been altogether denied; and this denial is most clearly seen in the new practice of referring to the group as a whole, and of describing human behaviour 'scientifically', from the outside, from the sociologist's standpoint. For behind this practice there lies the assumption that human history can be shown conclusively to be of a certain form. Choosing freedom now means choosing to rid ourselves of the impotence caused by living in a collective. Once we have formed a group, then choosing freedom means choosing to take steps to prevent its disintegration. And this can be assured only by our throwing in our lot completely with the revolutionary party.

It could be argued on the basis of *Being and Nothingness* that perhaps we should join the communist party, but that if we did, this might be our last free act. But now, if history can be shown to progress by a necessary and systematic dialectic towards 'the group', then even this act may not be free in any intelligible sense. We may be obliged to join the party by the forces of history. The conflict between freedom and the metaphysical necessity of things being as they are has broken out all over again. But the conflict is not now between my private freedom, which is part of my consciousness, and the necessities of the human predicament. It is a conflict between the freedom of a collection of people to settle its own affairs, and the ineluctable forces of the dialectical movement of history. In this context our freedom consists in intervention in the world of material things in a very special and limited sense. All we can do is to work on our physical environment to make things, which in their turn will control us and make us what we are. We are free to turn ourselves into tools or instruments of the forces of history. This is all we can do.

It is true that scarcity, which supplies the original motive to intervention, is said by Sartre to be a contingent feature of the world. It is, supposedly, possible to imagine a world without it; and in such a different world the course of human history would be different. But as things are, the economic condition of society determines, not our natures perhaps, but our development. To put in the proviso 'Things might be otherwise' does not provide us with any real alternative way of behaving, since things are *not* otherwise. Freedom, in a world of scarcity, is little more than a verbal concession to our sensibility. The contradiction between freedom and necessity which made ethics impossible in *Being and Nothingness* has not really been solved. For a new necessity has taken the place of the old.

Perhaps it should have been obvious right from the beginning that, for Sartre at any rate, an existentialist ethics must be impossible. His early passionate interest in human psychology looked as if it might lead to a moral philosophy; but in fact it never could. Still more clearly, an existentialist anthropology is an impossibility. For what must inevitably be lost is the notion of an intuited personal freedom with which Sartre's existentialism begins and ends. Whatever there may be to come in Volume II of the *Critique* in the way of social or political system-building, it is impossible that Sartre should go back to the viewpoint of *Being and Nothingness*. It would be wrong to judge that nothing constructive will come out of the *Critique*. But we have taken our leave once and for all of the private, compelling myth of the free man, experiencing his freedom in anguish, and faced with no necessity except that of choosing himself.

Short Bibliography

1 *Selected writings of Sartre*

L'Imagination, Paris 1936. Translated Forrest-Williams, University of Michigan Press 1962

Esquisse d'une théorie des émotions, Paris 1939. Translated Philip Mairet, Methuen 1962

L'Imaginaire: psychologie phénoménologigue de l'imagination, Paris 1940. Translated *The Psychology of Imagination*, Bernard Frechtman, London 1949

L'Etre et le Néant, Paris 1943. Translated *Being and Nothingness*, Hazel Barnes, Methuen 1957

La Liberté Cartésienne, Paris 1946

Saint Genet, comédien et martyr, Paris 1952. Translated *Saint Genet*, Bernard Frechtman, W. H. Allen 1964

Critique de la Raison Dialectique, Paris 1960 (Introduction—*Problem of Method*—translated Hazel Barnes, N.Y. 1964)

Les Mots (autobiography), Paris 1964. Translated *Words*, I. Clephane, Hamish Hamilton 1964

Situations, translated Benita Eisler, N.Y. 1965

2 *Historical background*

Article: 'Phenomenology', *Encyclopaedia Britannica*, 14th edition

Copleston, F. S. J., *Contempory Philosophy*, Newman Press 1956. (The second part of this gives a good survey of existentialist thought in general)

Chisholm, R., *Realism and the Background of Phenomenology*, Allen and Unwin 1956

Tucker, R. C., *Philosophy and Myth in Karl Marx*, Cambridge University Press 1961

Merleau-Ponty, M., *Phenomenology of Perception*, English edition, Routledge and Kegan Paul 1962 (especially the preface and introduction)

3 *Studies of Sartre*

Jeanson, F., *Le Problème moral et la pensée de Sartre*, Paris, Myrthe 1947

Murdoch, Iris, *Sartre, Romantic Rationalist*, Cambridge, Bowes and Bowes 1953. (An excellent discussion of Sartre's literary work in relation to his philosophy)

Cranston, M., *Sartre*, London, Oliver and Boyd 1962. (A useful short study of both the literary and philosophical work, with a full and excellent bibliography)

Laing and Cooper, *Reason and Violence*, Tavistock Publications 1964. (A discussion of Sartre's philosophy 1950–1960)

Joseph P. Fell III, *Emotion in the Thought of Sartre*, N.Y. 1965

Wilfrid Desan, *The Marxism of Jean-Paul Sartre*, N.Y. 1965. (Contains a useful exposition of the *Critique of Dialectical Reason*)

Index

185